Let the Children Give

Time, Talents, Love and Money

DELIA

DISCIPLES

PO BOX 340003 •
www.discipl

Cover design by Nanci Lamar.
Interior graphics by Melissa Glasgow

ISBN 13: 978-088177-501-3
ISBN 10: 0-88177-501-0

Library of Congress Control Number 2007921392

Printed in Canada.

Contents

Chapter One:

The Biblical and Historical Background of Stewardship

STEWARDSHIP FOR CHILDREN? Isn't that a little hard for them to grasp? After all, stewardship is just asking folks to meet the church budget. Or is it?

We have come to consider stewardship as a fancy way of asking people to pledge to the financial needs of the church, but it is far more than that. If we look at the true meaning of the word, we see stewardship in its entirety. Stewardship involves the whole of life, and that's why we need to begin early with stewardship training.

Ask a child for the definition of a steward, and he or she will likely say that a steward is a person who serves food and drinks on an airplane. Most adults in the church probably believe that the primary function of the stewardship committee is to raise money to meet the budget. Both of these definitions are partially right, but stewardship encompasses a much broader concept. In simple terms, a steward manages the affairs of another. Well-to-do persons in the past hired stewards who managed their households or estates.

As Christians, we are to act as stewards of all of God's affairs on earth—in fact, in the universe. God gives us abilities and talents so that we can accomplish this work. Paul reminds us of our gifts in 1 Corinthians 12, and in Romans 12:1-8 he reminds us that we must all work together, because we each hold an important role in Christ's mission.

With our abilities and talents, we can manage the earth. We can also manage our health, property, time, and relationships with others. In Jesus' parable of the talents (Matthew 25:14-30 and Luke 19:11-27), we learn that our talents are taken away when we don't use them. This is evident in churches where the sole focus is inward. When a church only concentrates on "raising the budget" to support buildings and programs, it loose its effectiveness in reaching others. In 1 Peter 4:10, we read, "Like good stewards of the manifold grace of God, serve one another with whatever gift each of you has received."

We are coming to realize that giving is as essential to the individual Christian as it is to the church body. We do not grow spiritually without giving, not just monetary giving but giving of all of our gifts. Therefore, we must focus not on the financial needs of the church, but on the spiritual need that God has embodied in each of us, the need for giving. This is stewardship: caring as God cares by using each talent that God has given us.

Biblical Background

Stewardship reaches deep into our biblical tradition. God took a formless void and made the earth. We were made in the image of God and entrusted with the care of the earth and all that is in it, from the ozone to the starving child. As caretakers of God's earth (and all that is in it) we are stewards for God. In both Leviticus (chapter 25) and Deuteronomy (chapters 8, 15, and 26) we read about God's gift of the earth and the importance of our caring for it. The precedent of the tithe, or of giving to God one-tenth of what we possess, is set forth in Deuteronomy 14:22. There are several psalms that speak of stewardship (Psalm 8:6-8; 24:1; 50:10-11, 12b). Ezekiel (18:4) and Haggai (2:8) remind us that God owns all things.

Matthew and Luke record parables that Jesus told about stewards. In Matthew 25:1-13, we find a parable that is often retold to remind us that we will not be included if we aren't prepared. The parable tells of ten bridesmaids, five who took their responsibilities seriously, and five who ignored their stewardship responsibilities. Jesus points out the importance of taking care of that which is our responsibility.

Jesus used a lamp to explain the importance of using our gifts in Luke 8:16-18. He said, "No one after lighting a lamp, hides it under a jar, or puts it under a bed, but puts it on a lampstand, so that those who enter may see the light. For nothing is hidden that will not be disclosed, nor is anything secret that will not become known and come to light. Then pay attention to how you listen, for to those who have more will be given;

and from those who do not have, even what they seem to have will be taken away" (NRSV).

In Luke 21:1-4 Jesus takes note of the people who were giving money in the Temple. One was giving much, but giving it for recognition. The other, a poor widow, gave out of love. Jesus made it clear that it was not the amount that was important, but the manner in which we give.

Jesus' statement about serving two masters (God and money) in Matthew 6:24 and Luke 16:13 makes it clear that our money is something that we should use as stewards, and that it should be used to serve God, our one true master. In Luke 12:31-34, Jesus again says that our heart is where our treasure is, implying that what we place as important is our master.

Even the story of the little boy who shares his lunch (John 6:1-15) indicates the importance of sharing what we have. The young boy willingly shared, and Jesus used the act as an example.

Historical Understanding of Stewardship

In the very early church, the Christians gave to each other without worry for themselves. They saw their role as caring for every person whom God placed in their paths, and even going out of their way to be stewards of God's people (Acts 2:44-45; 11:27-30).

The true meaning of stewardship got off track way back in the fourth century when Constantine declared the entire Roman world as Christian. This set the church up as an arm of the government, and the operating budgets of the churches were raised through taxes. The only need these churches had to raise money was to spread the gospel to other countries. Their routine "budget" was taken care of by the taxes of the citizens. This continued throughout Europe, where the government and church were united.

When Europeans came to North America they established a government that separated church and state. At first there were few problems about budgets. Most ministers were unmarried circuit riders, and as long as they had a horse and a couple of changes of clothing they managed fine. When they went to a community the members of the congregation saw to their housing and meals. The congregations usually met in schoolhouses or homes, and so there was no need to raise money for building upkeep.

But then things began to change. As communities became more established, they wanted pastors who were in residence, and they began to build houses of worship.

Suddenly they realized that the taxes no longer covered such items, and so there was a need to "raise a budget". This endeavor then became labeled "stewardship", and the broad scope of the word was lost. Our task today is to bring back the understanding of stewardship that was prevalent in the early church, the understanding that all that we have belongs to God, and as stewards we must recognize the mission of God as dominant in our lives (Acts 4:32-35).

Chapter Two:

Age Level and Learning Goals for Stewardship

I$_T$ $_{IS}$ $_{A}$ $_{CHALLENGE}$ $_{TO}$ $_{TEACH}$ stewardship to children. As noted above, we adults have a very stilted view of the word. But unless we start early, children will follow in the same stilted approach that all of us have held for many years. First and primary, adults working with children must set an example. Children generally want to follow the actions of adults. Once they become teens, or even pre-teens, they are less likely to imitate adults. And so we must set the pattern and habits of stewardship early, while the children are still receptive. Children pay attention to our actions, even when we don't realize that we are teaching them.

The church council needs to evaluate the approach it uses with stewardship. (See chapter ten for some suggestions for this.) When we throw recyclable items into the trash, and use Styrofoam cups for our coffee hour, the children receive a negative message about stewardship. Such actions say that a stewardship lifestyle is not important. Our actions speak louder than our words. As Jesus pointed out, our actions show where our heart is (Matthew 6:21).

There are many ways that children learn about stewardship, beyond simply having a stewardship lesson or two. Just as stewardship should be a lifestyle for individual Christians and for churches, it should be woven into the lesson plans and practiced during each study and event in the church. When they learn about the interlacing systems that God set up in the world, then children can recognize our role as stewards of the earth. When children learn that we recycle our drawing paper and take care of our toys at church, they experience stewardship firsthand. When they recognize that their parents give a percentage of their money to the church because God gave them the ability to make money, then they see stewardship as a part of their lives.

The committees and councils of successful churches cooperate and work toward common goals instead of operating in their own little boxes. Your children's council, stewardship committee, and church council can bring together the goals that will make a difference in children's stewardship lifestyle and consequently bring the church of the future to a more biblical understanding of stewardship. These goals, and this common venture, will improve the spirituality of the church and draw each member closer to God.

VERY YOUNG CHILDREN WILL:

- learn about the world in which we live in order to appreciate God's gift of the earth;

- build appreciation of themselves as a foundation for understanding how they can care for (be stewards of) God's world and God's people;

- learn to put their possessions away and care for them as God's stewards, and be called stewards when they act in this manner;

- grow as we praise them for their positive stewardship actions.

CHILDREN AGES THREE TO SIX WILL:

- enjoy songs, stories, and games about caring for the earth and for those around us;

- hear the word "steward" used in reference to those who care for the world and all that is in it;

- know persons who care for (are stewards of) various parts of our world;

- develop group skills that lead to a sense of being stewards and caring for others;

- grow in pride in the church family and recognize ways that the church acts as God's steward, caring for the world and helping the people of the world;

- appreciate the talents and abilities that God has given them;

- find simple ways to use their abilities to act as stewards, and be affirmed in those actions;

- recognize that we come together to worship and study and then go out to be God's stewards.

CHILDREN IN GRADES ONE TO THREE WILL:

- learn how their actions affect the earth and other people, and learn to accept responsibility for their own actions;

- enjoy expanded experiences with songs, games, and stories about caring for the earth and the people.

- learn to manage (be stewards of) their time;

- learn that money is a gift from God and belongs to God;

- recognize money as the product of ways we use our God-given talents;

- see different ways money functions in the church, learning how we need money for classroom supplies, cleaning materials, salaries, mission giving, etc.;

- expand understanding of acts of stewardship toward the world and others outside the church, and develop ways to express those acts.

CHILDREN IN GRADES FOUR TO SIX CAN:

- distinguish between independence and interdependence, recognizing that we are all dependent on the earth and interdependent among each other;

- recognize our responsibilities as a church member to act as a steward through prayers, presence, gifts, and service;

- develop specific talents to use as stewards;

- relate facts about the earth to the way we follow God's instructions to care for the earth and all that is in it;

- research and initiate conversations in order to find out about stewardship themselves;

- become aware of and carry out ways to practice stewardship through special projects and in everyday life.

In the following chapters you will find many practical suggestions to help you incorporate stewardship in all aspects of your ministry with children. Many of the activities began as seedlings, pruned and shaped by an interchange of ideas in the workshops I lead. Throughout my ministry they grew into healthy hybrids, ready to produce more seeds and spread across the fields of ministry. I encourage you to take these seeds and nurture them in your own mind and heart, so they burst into true opportunities for sharing stewardship, not just during a "Stewardship Campaign" but also throughout the year in your ministry with children.

Multiple Intelligences

God created each of us as individuals, and although we all use the same methods of learning, some of us learn best with certain methods, while others learn in different ways. Some of us are visual learners and some are audio learners. Therefore, it is important to use both visual and audio methods.

Several years ago Dr. Howard Gardner, an authority on the multiple intelligences that God gave each of us, wrote a book called *Frames of Mind: The Theory of Multiple Intelligences.* In it he identified the first seven intelligences listed below. Later, he added the eighth intelligence, nature.

Although these intelligences have been identified only recently, they have been around and a part of our learning process forever. Jesus used these methods in his ministry of teaching. He told stories, asked questions, used objects, involved his learners in fishing and washing feet, sang hymns, used small groups, spent time in prayer and reflection, and used illustrations from nature.

No one learns using just one of these intelligences, but sometimes we rely on one more heavily than others. That is why it is important to teach with methods that include several intelligences and to be aware of the methods that are most effective with each of the children you teach.

Verbal/Linguistic — has to do with language and words, both written and spoken.

Logical/Mathematical — has to do with inductive thinking and reasoning, statistics, and abstract patterns.

Visual/Spatial — has to do with visualizing objects and creating internal mental pictures.

Body/Kinesthetic — related to the physical, such as movement and physical activity.

Musical/Rhythmic — includes recognition of patterns, both tonal and rhythmic.

Interpersonal — deals with relationships between persons, including true communication.

Intrapersonal — primarily through self-reflection and awareness of that within us which guides us.

Nature — use of nature in learning.

Chapter Three:

Everyday Classroom Learning: Adding Stewardship to Regular Curriculum

WHEN WE TEACH WEEK AFTER WEEK, it is easy to let prime stewardship opportunities fall through the cracks. We fall into a rut of routinely grabbing the curriculum and collecting the supplies that the writers suggest, and hoping for the best. The first responsibility of preparing a lesson for Sunday morning, or any other event with children, is to go to God in prayer. This tunes us into the consciousness of God, and from that position we can work to create the proper atmosphere for sharing all aspects of our faith with our children.

We must train ourselves to consciously focus on experiences that point toward our responsibility as God's stewards. It may take a few weeks of conscious effort, but a stewardship lifestyle in the classroom can become consistent. Even with two-year-olds, we can make it a habit to pick up toys and return them to their proper place, thereby teaching stewardship of their toys.

Creating a stewardship lifestyle comes about through both curriculum and spontaneous opportunities. Part of this chapter will deal with weaving stewardship training into your regular curriculum, and in the rest of the chapter you will find additional opportunities to teach stewardship, both planned and spontaneous. Later chapters will give specific methods you may use for teaching stewardship.

Spontaneous Opportunities

Using Your Regular Curriculum

- As you use the Bible in your class, recognize the care we must take when we handle the book. We're careful not just because it is a special book, but simply because good stewards care for the books and other materials and equipment we use in the classroom.

- When a Bible story tells of how someone cared for part of God's world or cared for other people, mention the fact that the person acted as a good steward. (Examples include the shepherd, the Good Samaritan, the brother to the prodigal son, many of the rules established in the Old Testament, and such.)

- When scripture passage or stories in the curriculum mention things of nature, talk about our responsibility as stewards of God's earth.

- In a study on the church, speak of ways that the members of the church council are stewards of the money that people give, acting in ways that Jesus would.

- In a study about worship, speak of the offering as a way that we exercise stewardship of our money. When you look at the announcements in the bulletin, speak of ways that events exhibit stewardship and recognize our responsibility to use our time as good stewards.

Recognize Gifts

Each student has special gifts that God has given him or her. Take every opportunity that arises to recognize any special gift that a child has and comment on how he or she is a steward of those gifts. The special gift or talent may not be the artistic type of gift that we often call "talents". Instead, it may be the ability to excel in a subject at school, or to be able to make someone who is sad, happy.

Recognize Local Church Leaders

When a leader in the church is mentioned, recognize how that leader lives a stewardship lifestyle. Invite church leaders to visit the classroom, not only to talk about stewardship, but just so that the students will get to know him or her better. When the students know the leaders, they will observe the person and be more prone to follow his or her lifestyle.

Recognize Other Church Settings for Stewardship

Remember that learning will take place in many settings throughout the church. Think of ways you can connect your classroom experiences with worship, fellowship times, and other happenings in the church. An example of this might be when trees or shrubs are pruned, or if your church has a Christmas tree sale. When these plant products are put through a chipper, tell the children that the chips break down and provide nourishment for other plants. This is one way that we are stewards of God's earth.

Assign Stewardship Roles in the Classroom

Some classes assign specific "jobs" for "helpers" to do each week. Change your terminology, and use the word *steward*. Ask a child if he or she will be "Steward of the Crayons" this week. The person helping to pass out snacks becomes "Steward of the Snacks/drinks/napkins." Instead of simply asking children to erase the chalkboard, ask them to be "Stewards of the Chalkboard." (See "Create a Service Towel" in chapter four.)

Teach Spontaneously in Play/Activity Centers

Young children learn through play. Adults in play/activity centers in a classroom can be aware of the action and use spontaneous opportunities to teach stewardship. Do not do this in an instructional manner, but rather simply mention the action and affirm it or suggest some way that the child is acting, or has an opportunity to act, as a steward. Here are some examples:

- When a child does a caring act for a doll, say, "You care for the doll like a steward cares for other people."

- When a child is sweeping or washing play dishes, say, "You are acting like a good steward by sweeping/washing."

- When a child puts toys away, say, "You are a good steward of the toys."

- When a child makes a picture or builds a tower of blocks, say, "Your talent in drawing/building is a real gift from God. We are stewards for the talents that God gave us."

- When looking at a nature wonder center, ask, "Didn't God create a wonderful world? How can we act as stewards of God's world?"

Establish Classroom Stewardship Guidelines

Help children establish rules or guidelines for the classroom that practice good stewardship. To do this, ask the children what actions will help your class act as steward of what God has given us. Stress positive wording of the rules and guidelines. Instead of "Don't throw paper on the floor," suggest "Place used paper in the recycle bin." When the children set their own rules, they will help one another uphold the rules.

Experience Homelessness

This experience is appropriate for older elementary children with plenty of adult supervision and good security personnel. Plan an overnight event in the church courtyard or a fenced area. The children will dress in smelly clothing and sleep outside in a "city" constructed of large cardboard boxes. Before "bedtime" spend time discussing issues that homeless people face and our responsibility, as God's stewards, to help them.

Arrange for leaders from a local homeless shelter to talk to the children a week or so before the event, sharing some of their experiences and the circumstances of some of the people they work with. When the children realize that rich businessmen and women can lose their businesses and become homeless, and that the people in the shelters are still people, they loose their stereotypical vision of homeless people as bums.

You might publicize the event ahead of time and ask for pledges of money and articles of clothing. Decide how the pledge money and clothing will be used.

For security purposes, try to arrange for a police officer in plain clothes to spend the night with you. To add to the impact you can arrange for additional police officers, in uniform, to appear with flashlights just before dawn, instructing the "homeless" children to move on because they are loitering. The police officers may then rip up the boxes.

Be sure to allow opportunity for the children to discuss their impression of the experience. They might even write their new thoughts on homelessness for the church newsletter.

Distinguish Between Needs and Wants

Children learn language according to what we as adults accept and promote. Encourage children to distinguish between needs and wants by reminding them to use the term "I want" or "I would like" instead of "I need" in appropriate situations.

Using magazines and catalogs, ask the children to cut out pictures of items they like and need. Divide sheets of paper down the middle, labeling one side "I need," and the other side "I like." Discuss the children's pictures, and as they glue them on the appropriate side, help them understand which are needs, and which are things we'd like to have. Make a cover and fasten the sheets together with staples or a piece of yarn.

Learn Names of Plants and Animals

Use every opportunity available to learn the names of plants and animals. Also learn something about the life patterns and needs of the animals and the plants. When we know something by name and become acquainted with its needs, we naturally have more interest in caring for it. This makes stewardship even more appropriate.

Practice Recycling in the Classroom

There are many things that can be recycled in the classroom, from paper and crayons to water. Use both sides of a paper, and place any used paper that is not taken home in a recycle bin. Use paper or glass cups instead of Styrofoam or throwaway plastic. Learn the recycle symbol and make it a practice to look on the bottom of any plastic for the number that indicates how it can be recycled. You might even ask the students to search for the recycle symbol on items at home and assign a specific day that they will bring in anything they've found with the symbol on it.

As a class, investigate how the church office uses recycled paper and saves office papers for recycling. Encourage the use of the symbol on flyers and such when using recycled paper. If they are not recycling papers, perhaps your class can take on the project of taking it to a recycle location.

Set up the "R Rule."

Reduce
Reuse
Recycle

These three Rs bring about **R**esponsibility.

Planned Experiences

Create Stewardship Centers

Set up four ongoing centers in your classroom for children to visit at some time during each session. Make a sign with the following instructions for each center:

STEWARDS IN PRAYER

Write or draw something you thank God for, or a concern you have.

STEWARDS IN PRESENCE

Check your name off the attendance list.

STEWARDS IN GIFTS

Place your offering in the basket or your gift for others in the box.

STEWARDS IN SERVICE

Draw or write a way you cared for God's earth or God's people this week.

In a prayer time during the session, be sure to include the items of thanks and concerns that were written in the "Stewards in Prayer" center.

This helps the child make a practice of being a steward. It also lays a foundation for their future study of what it means to be a member of a Christian congregation. If children grow up practicing these acts and calling them stewardship, then we will change the congregation's understanding of the term.

Label Church Entrance

Make a sign for the church door: "Steward Entrance."

Make and Break Creation

This experience is appropriate for older elementary children. It will help them appreciate the importance of caring for something, and also the importance of recycling things after we use them. You will need materials that can be used to make, take apart, and remake something, such as blocks, clay, or pipe cleaners. The experience will be done with a partner.

1. Each person makes an individual "creation." After making the creating, each person tells the partner about the creation.

2. Partners then exchange creations, and each person tears the partner's creation apart.

3. Afterward, come together as a class and discuss:

   — How did you feel while you made your creation?

— How did you feel when you told your partner about your creation?

— How did you feel while you tore your partner's creation apart?

— How did you feel when you looked at your own creation after your partner had torn it apart?

4. Each pair works together to build a better creation, using materials from both of their destroyed creations.

Meet a Tree

I grew up in Florida among the spreading live oak trees. For many years, while my husband managed a district of the National Grasslands, our family lived in the prairies of the Dakotas. I grew to appreciate the subtle beauty of that country, though I did miss the massive trees of my childhood. On one occasion when we were traveling in a forested area, I enjoyed the trees so much that I actually wanted to stop the car and hug a tree! Since then, I often allow myself to "drink in" their beauty through my eyes. It's as if I can't get enough of looking at trees!

For this experience you will need to locate a place with several trees. (Note: be sure to warn the children about poison ivy and make sure they can identify it so they don't select a tree with the vine growing up the bark.) The children will do two things. First they will walk up to a tree, close their eyes, hug the tree and then spend time feeling the tree trunk. (You may want to provide blindfolds for this part.) Then they sit on the ground, far enough back from the tree to see all parts of it, and make mental notes of everything they observe about the tree.

Come together as a group and discuss these questions:

• Had you ever hugged a tree before? How did it feel to hug a tree?

• What was the texture of the tree? What did it remind you of?

• What did you find out about the tree that you didn't know before?

• What benefits do we get from trees? (Besides the obvious, be sure to include an esthetic value and an appreciation of God's world.)

• What can we do, as stewards of trees?

After this experience, you may want to arrange to plant a tree on the church property and act as stewards, watering and fertilizing the tree.

Newspaper "Forest"

Ask children to bring in old newspapers (or raid your church recycle bin). To create a "forest," stack newspapers around the room in four-foot-high piles. For each four-foot stack, one large tree had to be cut. After creating the stacks, count the number of trees cut down in order to produce the newspapers you brought into class. Return the papers to the recycle bin when you are finished. To make this result more visible, you may want to conduct the experiment in a courtyard, foyer, or fellowship hall, and use recycled green construction paper to make leaves for the newspaper "trees." Invite the congregation to visit your forest, informing them of the ratio of newspaper piles to trees.

Shopping Trip

Arrange for this ahead of time with a local grocery store. Divide the children into groups and assign hypothetical families of different sizes and life situations to each group. The number of children in a group does not need to correspond to the size of the family, but the group will decide what to "purchase" for that family for the week. One family might be a single parent with two children; one might be a retired couple living on a set income; one might be a family with teenagers; one might have babies to buy for.

Tell the students that their family has only $30.00 (or some other set amount). They are to make a list of what they would purchase with that money and act as good stewards of their money in the process. If possible, arrange for an adult to work with each group. You may recruit parents for this, thereby helping to educate the parents too. During the shopping the adult will guide the group as they discuss just what such a family will need, how much each item costs, and how to make the best choices nutritionally. They can distinguish between things that would be nice to have (wants) and things that are necessities (needs).

Stewardship Cookies

Use the following recipe for fortune cookies, but instead of inserting fortune papers in the cookies, insert papers that state ways we can practice our stewardship. The papers need to be ½ x 3 inches. Here are suggestions for statements on the papers:

> Be a steward: Conserve water.
> Be a steward: Recycle paper.
> Be a steward: Recycle cans, plastic, and glass.
> Be a steward: Choose wisely what to purchase.
> Be a steward: Give 10% of your earnings to God's work.
> Be a steward: Use your talents to work for God.

Be a steward: Make wise choices about how to use your time.
Be a steward: Pick up litter.

Ingredients:
2 large egg whites
pinch of salt
⅔ cup sugar
¼ teaspoon vanilla
1 cup flour
1 teaspoon instant tea powder
2 tablespoons water
6 tablespoons margarine, melted but cool

Method:
Mix the egg whites with the salt and sugar. Stir in, in this order: vanilla, flour, tea, water, and margarine. Mix well and chill thoroughly. Place on greased cookie sheet in small amounts, flattening into 3-inch circles. Bake at 350° for 3 to 5 minutes, or until edges turn brown. Quickly remove cookies from pan, place folded paper in center, bring edges up, and pinch together before cookie hardens. Cool. Encourage each child to share a cookie with someone outside the class and talk about the message in the cookies. Have everyone report back the next week.

Talent Stewards

Read or tell the story in 1 Kings 17:1-16 (the widow and her son who share meal and oil with Elijah) or John 6:1-15 (the boy who shares his loaves and fish). Tell about how these persons were stewards of what they had and shared it with others.

Give each person (teachers included) a piece of paper. Each person writes his or her name at the top of the paper and tapes it to his or her back. Everyone thinks of a special talent of each of the people, and then moves about the room, writing a talent on each person's paper. Remind the children that a talent is not necessarily something you perform. It might be what the child is good at in school, or it might be making a sad person happy.

If there are more than six or eight in the class, you might ask them to stand in a circle before they write the talents on each other's backs. Pair the children off (counting 1, 2; 1, 2). The pairs then face each other and take turns writing on each other's back. At a given signal, they face again, look at their partners, and repeat some common statement as a group (such as "Shalom" or "God made you great!"). Then they move forward one person and do the same with the next person, until each person has written on all of the backs.

Afterward, allow everyone to read their papers in silence, thinking about how they might be stewards of these talents and use them for God. You may play quiet music during this time. Discuss the talents in the class, and then have a prayer of thanksgiving for the talents.

Toy Fix-Up

Set a specific class time for everyone to bring a toy that needs repair. Ask the children to make certain the toy is repairable. Collect the toys, and then arrange for a future session when adults, preferably parents, can come to help repair the toys. This will help establish such a pattern at home. Work together repairing the toys so they may be used again instead of purchasing new ones. Speak of how we are stewards of our toys in this way, as well as stewards of our money by not having to purchase new toys.

Water Tap Count

All children can visualize the water taps in their homes. Younger children will need to tell you where the water taps are, and you can count them. Or you may make a mark, or draw a small water tap for each one they mention. After discussion of the many places in their homes where they can get water to drink, tell the children that many people don't have good water in their homes, and some don't even have clean water nearby. Sometimes the women and children must walk several hours each day, carrying water for their family. Older children who understand concepts of large numbers can begin to comprehend when you tell them that 1.2 billion people don't have water that is safe to drink.

Talk about rivers and lakes near your community. Specifically mention the source of the water that your community uses. Talk about how important it is to keep those waters clean and to conserve the water we use. Speak of being stewards of the water we use.

Ask them to try this experiment at home. You may want to write the experiment up and make copies for the children to take home.

Wash several gallon jugs (milk or juice jugs) clean. Each time you want to use hot water, save the cold water that comes out of the faucet (before it gets hot) in the gallon jugs. Keep track of how much water you waste by letting the water run just waiting for the hot water. Decide which times you might use the cold water tap instead of waiting for the hot water to run. Save the water in the jugs and use it to water plants or in the washing machine when you wash the clothes.

Chapter Four:

Art and Craft Activities for Stewardship

RECENT RESEARCH HAS POINTED OUT the fact that we all learn through varying experiences. These ways of learning have been labeled "Multiple Intelligences." (See page 12.) As leaders of children, we must provide a variety of ways for them to learn about stewardship. Children are exploring the various ways of learning and may not know which is best for them. They will have preferences, however it is important to encourage them to participate in all activities. Place your emphasis on the creating experience, instead of on the finished product.

Art and craft activities not only give children experience, but each time they see or use the object they made, they renew their feelings experienced during their learning. These activities will continue to reaffirm their learning of stewardship. Remember, we teach Christian education, not art. The activity acts as a method to reach our goals in teaching stewardship. Because of our product-oriented society, children learn to focus on their finished creation, rather than appreciating the creative process. As the children work, offer positive comments. You may simply say, "Tell me something about your picture. How did you feel as you were drawing it?" Encourage them to talk about their feelings, about the piece, and about the process.

As you display their creations in the classroom or elsewhere in the church, talk about how the art or craft item helps you think about our responsibility as stewards.

Develop pride in their ability to convey the theme, rather than their ability to produce an artistic piece. Remember that, although it is important to help children experience satisfaction in their work, rather than frustration, our goal centers on the learning, not the finished product.

Keep any display of the children's work current, replacing it with new creations. When items go home, encourage the children to talk with their families about what they learned. Help them recognize that they can use their creations to share what they learned about stewardship with others.

When selecting any of the suggested activities in this chapter, consider the abilities of your children. Have they developed eye-hand coordination? How do they handle scissors, glue, or pencils? As you plan to use a specific activity, first experiment with it yourself. Through experimenting with the activity you have a clear understanding of how the activity should be carried out. Although each activity in this chapter lists specific supplies, your experiment will enable you to be sure you have all the supplies and to better help the child. It will also produce an example for the children to see. If you have art talents similar to mine, then the children will look at your finished product and realize you do not expect perfection, only participation!

As I selected activities for this book, I cautiously avoided using food items unless such an item is to be eaten later. This is particularly important as we teach children about stewardship. When we tell children, on one hand, about people who starve because they have no food, and then turn around and prepare a craft or art object that uses food, we send a mixed message. Consider using small rocks, broken shells, twigs, bits of paper, old crayon shavings, broken eggshells, and colored sand (instead of beans, macaroni, or rice).

Wherever possible, help the children think of throwaway items that can be recycled for their projects. Encourage adults in your church to save such items, and arrange a place in your supply room to store them. You might advertise in your church newsletter for a volunteer to organize and maintain such a room. Consider the following wording in order to locate a person with this stewardship title:

> Do you enjoy seeing things in their proper place? Does it satisfy you to bring order out of chaos? Then organization is one of your gifts from God. Consider a ministry as steward of our supply room by calling _____.

As you make plans to use any of the activities in this book, recognize it as a learning tool. Acknowledge that you and the children are co-creators with God and are acting as stewards of God's world.

Badges or Bumper Stickers

Use some of these statements for your badges or bumper stickers:

> I (recycle symbol) Recycle.
> I am a steward of the world (or something specific).
> I (heart) the world and care for it.
> You're the solution to water pollution.
> Be a steward! Pick up and fix up.

Materials needed: Light-colored adhesive paper; marking pens (permanent markers work best for the bumper stickers).

Banners

Create banners with titles: "We are all stewards, appointed by God." or "A stewardship lifestyle requires constant awareness of God's world." Banners may be made from felt, recycled bed sheets, or another fabric. Decorate them with fabric crayons, colored markers, or tempera paints.

Materials needed: felt (bed sheet or another fabric) and fabric crayons (colored markers or tempera paints).

Bird Feeder

Several designs may be used for bird feeders. Cutting a large hole in one side of a gallon plastic milk container, about one inch from the bottom, makes the simplest. Be sure the cap is secure on the container. For hanging, make small holes on either side of the neck of the bottle, just below the cap, and thread a string or wire through the holes. Cover the bottom with seed and hang the bird feeder in the yard.

Or make a feeder by attaching a wire to a large pinecone for hanging. Then spread peanut butter on the pinecone and roll it in birdseed.

Materials needed: Gallon plastic milk container, or pinecone and peanut butter; birdseed; wire or string; scissors.

Bird Nest Supermarket

Use mesh bags from onions or other vegetables and fruits. Fill the bags with string, hair from a hairbrush, little bits of fabric or cotton, etc. Hang from a porch or in a tree. Sprinkle birdseed on the ground nearby to attract birds. Providing these nest-building materials is a way of being a steward, caring for the birds.

Materials needed: mesh bags; pieces of string, hair, cotton, bits of fabric, etc., birdseed (optional).

Decomposing Timeline

Using a large paper, make and illustrate a graph with the following information. You may prefer to make this on a bulletin board and fasten the actual objects to the graph.

Object	Time It Takes to Decompose
Test paper	2-4 weeks
Cotton t-shirt	1-5 months
Rope	3-14 months
Wool sock	1 year
Bamboo pole	1-3 years
Painted wooden board	13 years
Tin can	100 years
Aluminum can	200-500 years
Plastic 6-pack cover	450 years
Glass bottle	undetermined

(Based on information from *A-Way with Waste*, Washington State Department of Ecology.)

Materials needed: Large paper or bulletin board; markers or crayons.

Distribution of World Resources

Ask each child to divide a paper plate into three equal sections. In two-thirds of the plate, ask the children to draw six faces and put their name on one of those faces. Now ask them to draw ninety-four faces in the other one-third of the plate. Explain that the six faces represent the six percent of the world population that has one-third of the resources. Discuss how stewardship of your church or denomination's money is working to provide resources for those who have too few.

Materials needed: paper plates; pencils or crayons.

Fireplace Logs from Newspapers

This is a way of recycling newspapers and saving trees. Tightly roll small sections of newspapers around an old broomstick, one section after another. Before reaching the end of each piece, tuck another section in a few inches. When the log is two inches thick, slip it off the broomstick and tie the bundle with a light wire. These logs can be soaked (by adults only) in kerosene (never gasoline), in a tray made from a sheet of heavy-duty aluminum foil. Once the log has soaked up the fluid, wrap enough newspaper around each cord to make a five-inch thick log and tie it with a light wire. Three logs of recycled newspaper will burn all evening in a fireplace.

Materials needed: Newspapers; broomstick; light wire; kerosene (never gasoline); heavy-duty aluminum foil.

Light Switch Covers

Use plain colored adhesive backed paper, cut to the size of electrical switch covers. Using permanent markers decorate the covers, including a statement such as, "God's stewards turn lights off." Remove the backing and place on switch covers at church and at home.

Materials needed: Adhesive backed paper; permanent markers.

Litterbags

Decorate brown paper bags for children to take home for their families. Or you may make bags to distribute to the whole church. The litterbags may also be made from a large rectangle of heavy paper:

1. Hold the paper with the long side vertical. Fold and glue two inches of the top edge forward.

2. Fold bottom edge up to barely cover the glued section. Glue or tape this along left and right edges.

3. To hang, punch two holes, side by side, in the top two inches, and run yarn through the holes.

4. Decorate.

Materials needed: Brown paper bags or heavy paper; glue; tape; hole punch; yarn; markers or crayons.

Lunch Bags

Use old blue jeans to make lunch bags. These may be sold and the money used for missions, or you may give them away to church members when you stress the importance of recycling and living a life of stewardship.

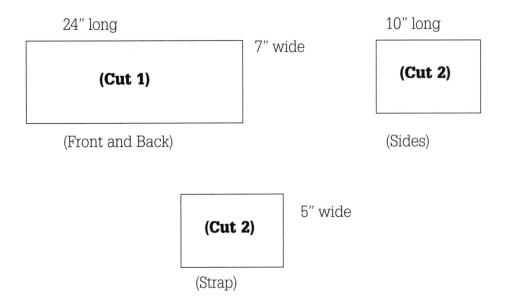

24" long

7" wide

(Cut 1)

(Front and Back)

10" long

(Cut 2)

(Sides)

5" wide

(Cut 2)

(Strap)

DIRECTIONS:

- Attach "side" pieces to the long sides of the "front and back" piece.

- To make straps, fold side of each strap piece in to the center line, and then fold again on the center line. Stitch the outside edges together.

- Turn the top of the bag down and stitch to form a hem.

- Attach a handle on each side of the bag and press the seams flat.

Mural of Church Stewardship

Using a large sheet of paper, make a mural that illustrates the ways your money helps your particular congregation carry on Christ's ministry. Include salaries, cleaning supplies and equipment, office supplies and equipment, electricity, water, phone, lawn-care equipment, gas for trips, vans to pick up the elderly, musical instruments, sheet music, curriculum, toys, Bibles, library books, hymnals, etc.

If you work with very young children, label the areas ahead of time and ask the children to illustrate various areas with pictures. Pictures may be drawn or cut out of magazines. Older children can interview leaders of the church and decide on which areas to label and illustrate.

Talk about how the stewardship of our money helps to carry on what Christ told us to do.

Materials needed: Large paper; crayons or markers, magazines, scissors, glue.

Nature Box or Sculpture

Discuss the importance of being stewards of nature as you create a nature box or sculpture. Ask children to bring items of nature from their own yards or take a field trip to collect items. Stress the importance of good stewardship through respecting the rights of other people and get permission to take nature items from their yards.

Working in teams, divide a shallow box with cardboard strips and glue the nature items in the box. Select a Bible verse about creation and glue this in the box also. (NOTE: See chapter three concerning using food for craft activities.)

Possible Bible verses: Genesis 1:1, 31; 8:22; Psalm 24:1; 50:11; 65:9; 66:5; 89:11; 147:7-9; Ecclesiastes 3:11a; and Song of Solomon 2:11-12.

Materials needed: Items from nature; glue or glue gun; shirt boxes or other shallow boxes; cardboard strips; scissors; marker.

Quilt, Rug, or "Sit-upon"

Old clothing can be recycled into a quilt, rug, or "sit-upon." Use the quilt as a covering for your worship center, as a wall hanging, or as a mat for outdoor events or storytelling.

Ask children to bring from home old items of clothing that may be cut up. Older children can cut these into squares; younger children may watch an adult cut them. Lay out the squares to make a design. The quilt can be hand stitched together, or bring a sewing machine into the classroom. As you stitch the fabric together, ask each child to bring his or her square to you when you need it. If you cannot bring a sewing machine into the classroom, you may collect the squares in the order that they were laid out and take them home for stitching.

Use the same procedure for making a rug. Tear the old clothing into strips. You may weave or braid the strips into a rug, or make a punch rug, using a canvas.

To make "sit-upons," use either squares or strips from the old clothing. Have the children exchange their pieces of fabric so each person has at least one piece from every member of the class. Then either piece the squares into individual small quilts, or make small rugs for "sit-upons."

As you work, talk about how we are stewards when we recycle our old clothes into items we can use.

Materials needed: Old items of clothing; scissors; thread and needles or sewing machine.

Sculpture Recycle

Ahead of time, ask children to bring discarded items from home, both recyclable and non-recyclable items. Work together in the class to make two sculptures—one of recyclable items and, one of the non-recyclable items. Put a smile on the recyclable sculpture and a frown on the other.

Materials needed: Discarded items; glue or glue gun.

Signs

Consider places on the church campus or in the homes that signs may be placed to remind people of ways to be good stewards. These might include:

- signs over sinks: "Good stewards turn off water while soaping hands."

- signs by classroom doors: "Good stewards turn off lights when leaving the room."

- signs for trash cans: "Good stewards put litter in trash cans."

- signs on grass near parking lot: "Good stewards do not park on the grass."

- signs by exterior doors: "Good stewards close doors to conserve heat and air conditioning."

Materials needed: poster or construction paper, markers, tape.

Steward Poster

Make a large poster of a "gingerbread-man" type figure. Ask the children to think of ways that different parts of the body can be a steward. Write these ways beside the appropriate body parts. Remind the children that stewardship involves our time and talents, as well as our money. Here are some examples:

Body Part	Stewardship Statement
Mouth	Eat an inexpensive meal and send extra money to those who need food.
	Sing about how we love God's earth and care for it.
Ears	Listen for opportunities to serve others.
Teeth and hands	Turn off water while brushing teeth.
Hands	Make bread or cookies for someone else, using a recycled container
	Prepare a box for the whole church to use for collecting food, and see that it is distributed.
	Fold newsletters for the church.
	Use cloth towels and napkins instead of paper ones.
	Compost natural kitchen waste.
	Turn out lights when not in use.
	Cut up plastic six-pack rings to protect animals.
Hands and legs	Pick up and recycle litter.
Feet	Participate in a walk-a-thon to raise money, and then decide how to use the money as a steward.

Materials needed: Poster board, markers.

Talent Search

Give magazines to each child. Give instructions to search for three pictures of things he or she does well and mount them on construction paper. (If they cannot find the right picture, they may draw one.) Explain that these things the children can do are talents, or gifts that God has given them. Talk about how good stewards use their talents in ways they know would please God.

Add the child's name to the paper and ask each child to tell about the pictures. After each child's statements, lead the class is saying together, "Thank you, God, for the talents you gave _____.

Materials needed: Magazines; construction paper; scissors; glue.

Towels of Stewards

Use John 13:1-17 to explain the symbol of a towel as an act of service. Explain that stewards serve others as they care for them.

On small towels, using fabric paints or permanent markers, illustrate ways that people serve. These might be individual towels, or towels might be made for the classroom.

Individual towels: Each week the child may illustrate one way that he or she served another person as a steward that week. At the end of a designated time, the children will take the towels home and share them with their family.

Classroom towels: Use the towels as a symbol of stewardship, to be worn by anyone acting as God's steward or as a server during a specific class period (such as the person responsible for putting away supplies or serving a snack). You may make a towel for each regularly assigned responsibility, using symbols for that responsibility. Make extra ones that simply say, "A steward of God." Keep belts in the classroom so that when a towel is worn, it may be looped over the belt.

Materials needed: Small towels or fabric hemmed on sides and frayed on edges; fabric paints or permanent markers.

T-shirts

Talk about how we can share our ideas with other people. Ask about t-shirts that tell different messages, such as telling what team you belong to or telling that you like a certain place, person, or movie. Ask for suggestions of things that might be put on a t-shirt to tell others what a steward does. Spend time helping children decide on their own messages before you begin the project.

Using white or light-colored plain t-shirts, children will create their own designs to express how stewards act. Use permanent markers or fabric paint. If you use fabric crayons they must be ironed on the wrong side after completing the design. Place a sheet of cardboard inside the t-shirt, under the fabric you are working on.

Materials needed: White or light-colored plain t-shirts; permanent markers, fabric paint, or fabric crayons and iron.

Chapter Five:

Drama, Storytelling, and Reflection Activities for Stewardship

IF WE ARE TO HELP CHILDREN develop a stewardship lifestyle, then we must approach the process in ways that they learn best, recognizing the multiple intelligences that fulfill our learning needs. Drama and storytelling satisfy requirements of children who are verbal/linguistic and body/kinesthetic learners.

Today, children are whisked from one activity to another and spend much of their at-home time before the television or computer. They seldom have opportunity to simply think about things. The intrapersonal intelligence, important for our spiritual development, is seldom cultivated. It would do us well, as teachers of children, to build into each session a quiet time for reflection. The soul can only run on high energy for so long.

Storytelling

As a teaching method, storytelling dates back to the beginning of time. The parent's knee or the campfire gathering set the early stages for storytelling. In Deuteronomy chapters four and six, the people are told to pass God's commands on to their children by talking about them " . . . when you are at home and when you are away, when you lie down and when you rise." The stories of the Old Testament were first shared orally with no written versions. The stories that later became the gospels also had their origins as oral tradition. We have no records of these stories being written down until about forty years after Jesus' death.

Jesus used storytelling when he taught through parables. Sometimes he used storytelling with individuals or an intimate group, and sometimes he told stories to a large gathering. He didn't always give the listeners the "moral" of the story. Most often he let the story stand on its own and sink into their hearts at the right moment.

We usually think of storytelling as simply sitting in front of someone and telling or reading a story, but storytelling comes in many forms. One style of storytelling may appeal to your class more than another, but don't hesitate to try new ways. And remember that every child in your class will not respond in the same manner to each story form. Storytelling helps us live through other people's situations and develop an understanding through their experiences. It also helps us work through possible actions that we might take in given situations.

Becoming a Storyteller

Anyone can tell a story, but most of us need some help in developing our skills. The way we tell a story makes a difference in how it is received.

Turn to Luke 12:13-21 and read the story of the "rich fool" twice. First read verse 20 as if God were passing judgment. The second time, read it with compassion. As you will see, without the tone of the storyteller's voice, we do not comprehend the full meaning of the story.

As we work with scriptures, we must realize that much of the original passages had no punctuation. For example, the King James Version of Psalm 121 used a period at the end of the first verse. Later translators changed the punctuation to a question mark because they realized that all of the hills surrounding the psalmist would have had pagan altars built on the top of them. And so, the translators saw the psalmist's words as a question about where his help came from – not from the pagan god of the altars on the hills, but from the one true God.

A storyteller not only uses the words, but he or she must understand the story well enough to interpret just what is meant. The tone of voice, facial expressions, and body language all go into storytelling.

All stories contain plot, place, and persons. Like the legs of a milking stool, we need all three to make the story complete. We often think of the plot as the most important, but sometimes the plot is developed only to tell about the person or the place. Without the descriptive words, a story falls flat.

The following suggestions will help you learn a story:

1. Identify the four parts of the story (introduction, plot, climax, ending).

2. Get to know the characters, the customs of the time and area, and the location of the story.

3. Think about how the listener will relate to the characters and situations in the story.

4. Divide the story into blocks. Concentrate on each block, and look at the connecting words between the blocks. Concentrate on the beginning and end of each block, then on the whole story.

5. Repeat the story several times, "thinking" it as you speak. You will want to internalize the story—help it "leave" the page and become a part of you. Some people find it helpful to use a tape recorder as they practice. A storytelling partner will also help. Consider these suggestions as you tell the story:

    a. A well-told story is better than a well-read story, but a well-read story is far better than a poorly told story. The key lies in knowing the story so well that it becomes a part of you, whether you tell it or read it. If you only use the book to follow the sequence, then write the sequence on a large sheet of paper and post it high on the wall above the listeners' heads. You will remember the sequence more easily if you practice it in blocks.

    b. Consider any props and gestures you plan to use. These enhance the story. But any story should always be told as if the listeners could not see the props and gestures. Use only appropriate gestures. In the story of Jesus healing the paralytic, Jesus asked the scribes, "Why do you raise such questions in your hearts?" If an accusing, pointing gesture is used, then one message will be conveyed. But if a gesture of opening the hands in puzzlement is used, then we see Jesus' question in another light, as concern over the scribes' attitude (Mark 2:1-12). Which attitude stands more in keeping with Jesus' life and teachings?

    c. Think about your tone of voice, facial expressions, and body posture. Happiness comes about through the tone as well as the words.

    d. Don't avoid pauses. Pauses give us time to think. They allow space in our thoughts for setting the stage.

6. Relax and enjoy the story. You will find that storytelling can bring you as much joy as it brings the listeners. (These suggestions adapted from Delia Halverson, *How to Train Volunteer Teachers* [Nashville: Abingdon Press, 1991], Handout 12.)

When we use storytelling in teaching we need to give opportunity afterwards for the students to reflect on the story. If the story parallels a scripture, be sure to read the passage as you begin the discussion. Here are a few questions you might ask:

- How did you feel about the story?

- With which characters in the story could you identify?

- Did the characters do what you expected them to do?

- How might the story have been different if the characters had acted differently?

- What did you learn from the story?

Storytelling need not be biblical. You may draw from history, use stories from today, or even use pretend stories. A story might be about a foolish choice that a child made with his or her money or time. It might be a modern day paraphrase of a Bible story. Here is an example of a modern day paraphrase of the story that Jesus told about a master and three servants (stewards) in Matthew 25:14-30.

God's Gifts

Esther enjoyed running and heard about a marathon race at her school. She signed up for the race and burst across the starting line with high energy. After the first few blocks, however, she realized that other racers were catching up with her and she was falling behind. Her energy seemed to disappear. She did manage to finish the race, but she was among the last straggling racers to cross the line.

The loss of the race, however, didn't dampen Esther's spirit. She began training right away for the next race. She learned that running a slower, more even pace helped her conserve her energy and she was able to run farther in a shorter time. In the next race she entered she finished in the top ten, and after several months of practice she actually won a marathon!

Ricardo, another student in the same school, spoke English as a second language. He dreamed of being a leader and standing before his class. But each time he read his report before the class his knees shook and the words stuck in his throat, coming out with such an accent that the other students giggled.

One day Ricardo began talking to himself in front of his mirror. He said, "Why can't you be more confident when you stand before the class?" As he talked to himself in front of the mirror his words came easier and easier. Soon he became accustomed to his own voice and volunteered for the next assignment. Day after day he read his report in front of the mirror. When the appointed day arrived, Ricardo stood before the class and imagined he was at home in front of his own mirror. He read the report without a hitch, and his English was perfect! Two years later he stood before the student body and thanked his classmates for electing him president.

There was a third student in that school named Lois. She wrote a short story for an English assignment. The teacher liked the story and read it before the class. She said, "Some day this student will be an author." Lois dreamed of autographing books and earning fat royalty checks. When the next assignment was given, Lois decided that she was such a good writer that she didn't need to spend much time on the assignment. She played computer games all evening and wrote a story as she rode the school bus the next morning. As a result she received a poor grade and decided that writing was too hard. She never became a writer. In fact, the writing ability she had before seemed to dry up. The words no longer "wrote themselves."

Many communities have a Storyteller's Guild. Check your library for information on local organizations that encourage and assist storytellers. They can help you set up a storytelling workshop for leaders who want to become more proficient. Consider contacting the Network of Biblical Storytellers (NOBS) at www.nobs.org.

Books

Keep a watchful eye for children's books that encourage stewardship. A book doesn't have to be religious to be useful in studying stewardship. Use picture books of different parts of the world with young children. After reading a book you can easily speak of how God gave us the world and we are stewards and must care for God's world. A book about a child learning how to use his or her money (or misusing it) can easily be turned into a learning experience in stewardship by asking how the child was or wasn't a good steward of the money.

Make Pretend Stories

Collect pictures from magazines that show good or bad stewardship of our natural resources, toys and other possessions, and money. Ask the students to choose a picture and then make up a story that might go with it. Young children will need an adult to write their story. Share the stories with the church family.

Shared Storytelling

For children who can read, mix up parts of a story about stewardship, and then have each child read his or her section. Here are suggestions on how you can mix up the sections of the story:

- Write sections of the story on strips of paper and insert each strip into a balloon. Standing in a circle, toss the balloons back and forth. On a signal, each person takes a balloon and pops it. Then the children read their section of the story to themselves and find where they fit into the story according to the other children's strips of paper. When all have found their places, read the story aloud in sections.

- Write sections of the story on strips of paper, number them, then mix them up and pass them out. Children then arrange themselves in the order of the numbers and read the story.

- Write sections of the story on strips of paper for a treasure hunt. On the back of each strip, write a clue for where the next section of the story will be found.

Reflection

The world of children today is filled with some sort of information being fed to their brains. It may be television, car radios, cell phones, or some sort of personal listening device. We condition our children to think that every void must be filled from without. They have little opportunity to fill their voids by listening to God's voice within themselves.

After the people of Israel crossed the Jordan River into Canaan God told them to gather twelve large stones from the place that the ark crossed, representing the twelve tribes, and put them down at Gilgal, the place where they spent their first night in the promised land. The people were instructed, "When your children ask in time to come, 'What do those stones mean to you?' then you shall tell them that the waters of the Jordan were cut off in front of the ark of the covenant of the Lord. When it crossed over the Jordan, the waters of the Jordan were cut off. So these stones shall be to the Israelites a memorial forever." (Joshua 4:6-7) This created opportunity for reflection, for remembering what God had done for them and that they belonged to God.

Jesus encouraged the listeners to reflect on what he taught. His suggestion for private prayer in chapter six of Matthew suggests reflection, and he practiced going apart to reflect and communicate with God. We find reference to this in Matthew 14:22-23; 26:36-43; Mark 1:35; 14:32-39; and Luke 5:15-16; 6:12-16.

Do not worry about allowing silent times in your classroom. Children need that time for reflection. God cannot talk to us when our minds try to fill up every void moment.

The following experiences will help children reflect. Be alert to other situations in your regular curriculum where you can allow some quiet time for reflection.

Borrowed Items

Reflect on and/or discuss the situations below:

- How would you feel if your little sister colored on your mother's library book, and your mother made you buy a new one?

- How would you feel if you marked on your own library book, and you asked your mother to pay for a new one?

- How would you feel if your friend borrowed your roller blades, left them outside, and the friend's dog chewed them up?

- How would you feel if you left your own roller blades outside and your dog chewed them up?

- How should we treat borrowed things? Read Psalm 24:1. What does it say about the ownership of the world? What does this mean about being a steward?

Creating Something Special

Guide children's thoughts by asking them to close their eyes and think as you read the following:

Imagine that you have a special mission. You are about to create the most beautiful thing in the world. Think what that special thing might be. (Pause) All right, now keep that in your mind and imagine that you are creating it. (Pause) Imagine the care that you take as you make it. (Pause)

Now, it's all made. Imagine that you place it on a shelf in front of you and look at it. Isn't it wonderful? (Pause) Suddenly you think that something might happen to it. What do you suppose might happen to it? (Pause)

You really don't want something to happen to it, so whom might you get to take care of it? (Pause) Think about the person you would ask to care for this special creation. That person would be your steward. Do you think he or she would understand how important this creation is to you? (Pause)

God made something special when God made the world. Here is what the psalmist said about how God found someone to take care of this special creation:

You have given them dominion over the works of your hands; you have put all things under their feet (Psalm 8:6).

Tell the children to open their eyes and talk about how they felt about their great creations, and their fear of having them destroyed. Remind them that we are stewards of God's creation, stewards of the earth.

Fable of the Sticks

Collect small sticks, all about the same size and small enough for a child to break. You may use craft sticks for this. Give each child two sticks and ask them to break one stick. Say, "I wonder what will happen if we combine our sticks."

Collect the second stick from each child and make a bundle, binding them with a string or rubber band. Pass the bundle among the children, challenging them to try to break the sticks now. Then read the following fable:

> Once there was a man who lived on a farm with his seven sons. There was much work to be done on the farm, and the seven sons were responsible for the work. They had to take care of the animals, and they had to take care of the land. They were the stewards of the family farm.
>
> But the sons did not work together. One son would say, "That's not my job! Someone else can fertilize the corn." Or another son would say, "I'm tired of caring for the cows. I'd rather go and play baseball." They constantly quarreled among themselves, and the animals suffered and the land produced very little food.
>
> The father had trusted the care of the animals and the land to the seven sons, and so he called them all together. He gave each son a stick and told him to break it. This they did easily. Then the father took seven more sticks and bound them together. He handed a bundle to each son and told him to try to break it now. The first brother took the bundle eagerly and tried to break it, but couldn't. Then each brother, in turn, tried to show his superior strength by breaking the bundle, but none were able to do it as long as the sticks were all bound together.
>
> Then the brothers realized that there was strength in working together. They saw that they must work in peace in order to accomplish the job of caring for the animals and the land. They realized that stewardship is not a job for just one person, but for everyone.

Methuselah, the Tree

Reproduce page 47 that shows the cross section of a tree. Give each child a copy and a pencil, and ask them to think about your words as you tell them about the tree, Methuselah, and to follow your instruction. (For younger children, write the sentences they are to write on a board or have them printed out and cut into strips so that the children can tape or glue the strips at the appropriate places.)

Read the following, pausing for them to write the statements on the tree rings. After you finish, use their papers as they dedicate themselves to act as stewards for God. A suggestion for the dedication service follows the story.

I Am Methuselah, the Tree

My name is Methuselah. I am a bristlecone pine more than 4,600 years old, one of the world's oldest known living things. I grow in the Inyo National Forest in the White Mountains of California. I'm bent by the winds that have blown all these years, telling me of the many changes in our world.

You may think I'm old, but many, many years ago, even before I sprouted from a seed, God set this earth into systems so that all the world works together. Sometimes we humans call the systems that God set up *ecosystems*. Look at the picture of my rings, and in the ring in the center, write the sentence, "Ecosystems created by God." That's spelled e-c-o-s-y-s-t-e-m-s. This happened before I sprouted from a seed. (Pause)

You see, a part of the ecosystem includes the way you humans must have oxygen to breathe, and we trees must produce oxygen as we grow. We are all in this together, making the world function in the way God planned.

As I grow, each year I put on a new ring. Look for the wide ring closest to the center ring. That represents the ring that grew when I was well over a thousand years old. That is when someone wrote the book in the Bible called Genesis. The stories in Genesis had been told over and over around campfires and in homes. Now someone wrote them down. The writer wrote that God created human beings in God's own image. God gave to the Hebrews, and to all people after them, dominion over the earth. Dominion over something does not mean that you can use it any way you want, but it means that you must be responsible for it. You must be stewards of it. That makes you stewards of the earth and all that is in it. Write in that ring, "Writer of Genesis tells us that people are stewards of God." (Pause)

People did not always care for the earth. The next ring represents the time Moses taught the people to care for God's earth by letting the land rest one year in seven. Write in that ring, "Moses tells us to let the land rest one year in seven." (Pause)

The next large ring represents the years that King David lived. He wrote many psalms or poems about the earth. These are in our Bible. One of them says, "The earth is the Lord's and all that is in it, the world, and those who live in it" (Psalm 24:1). In that ring on the tree, write, "David tells us the earth belongs to the Lord." (Pause)

You will find two more large rings in your picture. The next to the last ring represents the years that Jesus lived on earth and taught about caring for the earth and the people. Write in that ring, "Jesus taught to care for God's earth and people." (Pause) In order to care for God's people, you must care for the earth, so that God's people have a good place to live. If we don't care for the earth, the people in the future won't be able to live well.

You will see many tiny rings between the ring for Jesus' life and the outside of my trunk. In those years, some folks have cared for the earth and God's people, and some folks haven't. The space closest to the bark on my trunk represents this year. If you want to be a steward for God and care for God's earth and people, write in that ring, "I will be a steward and care for God's earth and people." (Pause)

Dedication of Stewards

Leader: God gave us the authority to care for the earth.

All: This made us stewards of the earth and all that is in it.

Voice 1: We are responsible for the animals on the earth.

All: We must care for the animals because they were placed here by God.

Voice 2: We are responsible for the people on the earth.

All: We must care for all people because God created us in God's likeness to be caring people.

Voice 3: We are responsible for the plants and water on the earth, and the air that surrounds our earth.

All: We must care for the plants and the water and the air because without them our earth cannot function.

Leader: Our God, we know that at times we have not been good stewards of your world.

All: We regret our actions of the past. We ask your forgiveness.

Leader: We dedicate ourselves to follow your charge to act as stewards. We want to become better stewards of your world and all that is in it.

All: We place these tree rings before you to signify our decision to act as your stewards. Amen.

Song: "A Charge to Keep I Have." (You will find this song in most hymnals.)

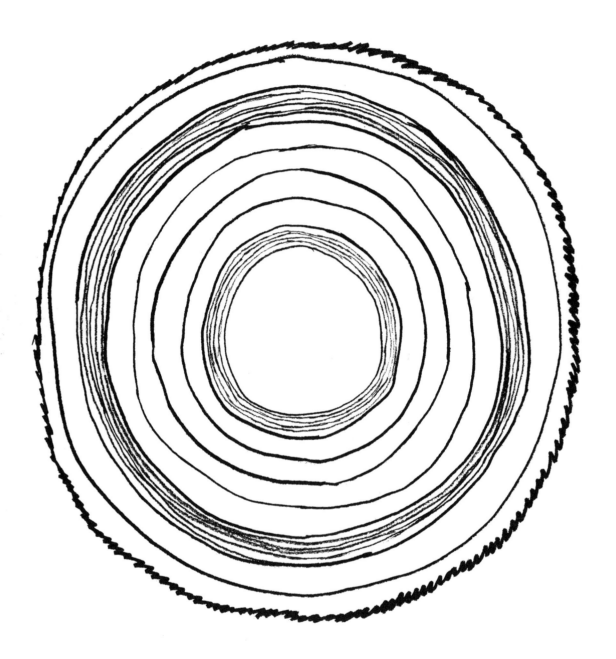

Order Out of Chaos

This is appropriate for older children. Before class time, create chaos in the classroom by upsetting the chairs and tables, moving things out of place, throwing "clean" trash on the floor, and so on. Leave an open area near the door so that all of the class can sit together on the floor. Close the blinds or cover the windows, and turn off the light. Meet your students outside the classroom and read (or have a student read) the first chapter of Genesis. Then take the children into the classroom and sit together on the floor in the dark.

Recall that before creation, the world was without light, was void of life, and without form. Then ask the students if they remember what God did the first day of creation. When someone responds, "light," flood the room with lights. Ask the students how the room is different. Talk about the definition of *chaos* in comparison to *order*. As the class goes about setting order to the room, talk about the order that God has established in the universe, that one thing depends on another, and some things are becoming extinct or damaged because we have not been good stewards and the balance has been upset. Discuss our stewardship responsibility to maintain the balance God created.

Drama

It would be hard to imagine Jesus and the twelve disciples producing a large dramatic pageant, but we can't say that Jesus' life was void of drama. Many events in his life are about as dramatic as they come, such as walking on water, washing feet, and a symbolic meal. The difference in Jesus' drama and that of an organized children's playhouse theater is that he created drama that was personal and more than a spectator sport. He totally involved the learners.

It is important for us to realize that when we use drama to teach children about stewardship our goal is not a polished performance. In fact, we must get away from seeing drama as performance, but rather as a learning tool for the children. In the classroom we try to involve as many of the children as possible in the drama. The best use of drama in Christian education benefits the participant more than the spectator.

Clowning

Clowning by an adult for children can be a way to present a message about stewardship. People who work with clowning in the church usually say they benefit from the preparation of the activity more than those for whom they are clowning, and this is what we want for our children. We want them to benefit from the experience of clowning. Clowning offers children an ideal opportunity to express feelings that they might not ordinarily feel comfortable revealing. Use clowning to help children express ways they can be stewards and the happiness that a person experiences when we use our talents and act as stewards, caring for God's world and the people in the world.

You don't need costumes or face makeup to use clowning in the classroom. Ease a group into clowning by asking everyone to act as a clown would act. Remind them that clowns express their feelings through their facial expressions and actions, rather than with words. Ask the children to use their faces and/or actions to express:

1. A happy feeling, being playful and bouncy.

2. An unhappy feeling, with a sad face and droopy walk, perhaps like a wilting flower.

3. Unsure of self, falling down and tripping over things. (See precaution below.)

With older children, you may identify these three basic types of clowning as white-face, sad-face, and Auguste clowns. With all ages, simply state that we can use these actions in different ways to express our feelings.

A word of caution: Use the third type of clowning only if it applies directly to your situation. This can be taken as a way to poke fun at the disadvantaged. I would suggest that the class usually work with the first two methods. In all cases, be sure to follow the negative feelings (droopy, unhappy, clumsy) with positive feelings (happy, playful, bouncy), after God's people act as stewards.

Creative Movement

Give children permission to use body movements to express their feelings, as long as it is not harmful to themselves or others. Most young children feel comfortable using their bodies to express feelings. This is evident in the tantrum of a two-year-old or the exuberant jumping of any preschooler.

Creative movement begins when we free ourselves to move. Before any experiment with creative movement, spend some time relaxing the body and expressing movement freely. Simple games and exercises, such as the following, help us relax:

1. Act like a boat floating in water, or a kite, bobbing in the wind.

2. Act like a kitten asleep on a rug, who begins to wake and stretch.

3. Walk in different ways, such as jerky, smooth, stiff, floppy, light-footed, heavy-footed.

4. Sitting on a chair or on the floor, use the top part of your body as if it were a hammer.

5 Act like a flower, slowly opening its petals. (Adapted from Delia Halverson, *New Ways to Tell the Old, Old Story* ([Nashville: Abingdon Press, 1992], p. 36.)

After children feel comfortable about movement, ask them to use their bodies to express certain stewardship situations. Or tell a story, and at specific times during the story, ask them to use movement to dramatize it.

Older children can express more abstract forms. When you have worked with movement for a while, the older children can develop specific motions to accompany hymns or readings. Arrange for them to use these in congregational worship to help convey the message of stewardship. They may use the motions while the congregation sings a hymn. The flowing motions may help them begin:

Words/Feelings	Actions
loving	hands to heart
joy of stewardship acts	clap hands or rapid motion of hands upward
resisting the urge to not act as stewards	pushing hands down to side and back
inclusiveness of all in congregation	extend hands and move them from center to sides
peace/love flowing from us as result of actions	arms outstretched

Echo Pantomime

If you have never used echo pantomime in your class, explain it briefly. Tell the children you will tell a story or say short sentences that include some action. After each sentence, they will repeat (echo) the sentence and action together. Older children can help create echo pantomime themselves and lead younger children in the activity. Here is an example:

God's Stewards Care

Words	Actions
God's people are stewards in many ways.	Spread out arms and smile.
Sometimes we plant new trees.	Pretend to dig in ground.
Or pick up trash along the roadside.	Pick up trash.

When we wash our hands, we are careful to save water.	Pretend to wash hands.
We care for the animals.	Pretend to pet an animal.
Sometimes we care for small children.	Squat down as if small.
Or we listen to older people.	Cup hand behind ear.
We pray for those who are sick or in need.	Hands in prayer.
Sometimes we write letters.	"Write" on hand.
Or give our money to the church to help others.	Put money in offering.
Sometimes we hammer nails.	Pretend to hammer.
Or even paint a house.	Use imaginary paint brush.
You and I are all God's stewards.	Point to someone else and then self.
God's stewards care.	Spread out arms and smile.

News Alive!

Bring newspapers to class and divide the children into groups of three or four. Each group looks through a newspaper and selects an article that tells of someone being a good steward. They will pantomime the story or create a human sculpture that depicts the news story. Then someone in the group tells briefly what is in the article. To do this in a shorter time, you may select several articles ahead of time and distribute them.

Open-ended Story

Give out slips of paper, each with a positive or negative answer response. Tell a story about someone who must decide to be a good steward, but stop the story before the conclusion and ask students to finish the story by following the instructions on their paper. Discuss what might happen if they actually did that. Discuss the best response and any additional good responses they might make. Here is a sample story with possible responses:

> Peter was on a field trip with his class. Peter had looked forward to this hike in the state park for a long time, ever since the teacher first announced it. The day was perfect, and he wore his hiking shoes and had his snack packed away in his backpack.
>
> When they got to the park, the park ranger met with them and told them about the history of the area. He explained that the ground was very thin, and the trees that grew there were special trees because they did not require deep roots. He talked about how certain trees adapted themselves to the circumstances of their environment. Then the park ranger

explained the rules of the park. He said that they had set up the rules in order to protect the environment. As they went on the hike they were to stay on the trail and not disturb the ground beside the trail or remove anything. They were also told not to leave any litter around when they had their snack.

During the hike their teacher pointed out different plants along the way. Some of them were plants they had studied in class and some were new to them. When they reached an area with a picnic table, they took a break for their snacks. As Peter began to get his snack out of his backpack he noticed that two of his classmates were sitting on a soft mossy piece to ground, away from the designated picnic area.

Possible responses:

- Tell someone in charge.

- Remind the persons of the rules.

- Scold the persons for disobeying the rules.

- Turn the other way and pretend not to see the students.

- Join the group of students.

- Wait and tell the park ranger later.

- Ask the group of students to join you inside the designated picnic area.

Pantomime

Children take turns pantomiming ways they can be good stewards. Class members guess the act from their actions. Ahead of time, select common symbolic motions to indication whether the act might be "at home," "at school," "on the street" or "at church."

Puppets

Puppets have become very elaborate, with stages and prepared scripts. Such puppets may be purchased in stores or through supply catalogs. This style of puppet show is just that, a show. There is very little participation by the children beyond some response to questions or simply feeding back what the puppets tell them to say.

The best puppet dramas involve children everything, from making the puppets to imagining what the puppet will say. This uses several learning styles and enhances creativity. It has been proven that the best learning happens when we are involved in the actual teaching. By planning their own drama with puppets, the children are learning in this manner.

Children enjoy puppets that are easily made, using a sock, a fabric cut with a simple head, arms, and body, or a paper bag.

A simple face puppet, glued or stapled to the end of a craft stick or a strip of heavy cardboard, is appropriate for stories that express feelings. Have each child make a stick puppet with a smiling face and one with a sad face. During the story or discussion the children will exchange the puppets, depending on the feelings expressed.

Try a new experience by bringing a sewing machine into the classroom to put together fabric puppets, after the children have drawn the faces and clothing with colored markers. You can also make a hand puppet from a stuffed toy by opening a seam and removing the stuffing from the body, and a little from the head and arms (or front legs), to allow fingers to be used.

If you use puppets to tell a story it is not necessary to have a puppet for each character. Children who do not have puppets with "speaking parts" can be puppets in a crowd. Or you may simply use one puppet to tell the story.

Many children will make up stories or express feelings about a situation when they can speak through the puppet, instead of saying it directly themselves. Or the child may pretend that the puppet "whispers" the information into the ear of the child, and the child speaks for the puppet.

Although it is not necessary to have a stage for a puppet, you may turn a table on its side and have the children sit behind the table and hold the puppets above the edge of the table. Or you might tie a rope across part of the room and drape a blanket over the rope, hiding the children as they manipulate the puppets above the blanket. Be certain that there is plenty of room behind the stage area for children to move about. Some of the purchased puppet stages can cause crowding if more than one or two children work behind them.

Signing

Signing has specific movements for specific words or phrases. Because it is the language for the hearing impaired, it should be learned correctly. Help the children distinguish between signing and creative movement. They will enjoy both experiences.

With preschool children, use only an occasional word. Older children can learn a complete song or reading. You might ask someone with signing experience to translate a song that you sing frequently or a theme song for a study on stewardship. Either learn the signing yourself or arrange for the signer to teach the children. You may also video-tape the signer and use the tape to teach the children.

Stop-action Drama

A stop-action drama allows students to concentrate on sections of the story, thereby enabling them to more thoroughly digest it. Students will decide on ways to show a part of the story in still-life scenes that stop the action.

This method of drama can be used with most stories. As an example, the story of the boy who gave his lunch to Jesus (John 6:1-15) can be stopped for still-life scenes:

- at the end of verse 4 – Jesus and disciples sit together;

- at the end of verse 9 – Andrew standing with the boy and the boy handing lunch to Jesus;

- at the end of verse 11 – everyone sitting in groups and Jesus blessing bread and fish;

- at the end of verse 13 – some children as disciples, taking up leftover food in baskets.

After the story is complete (verse 15), encourage the children to reflect on how the young boy was a steward by sharing his lunch.

Chapter Six:

Writing and Research Activities for Stewardship

AS I TEACH JOURNALING COURSES I realize that hesitant adults to put thoughts on paper. Perhaps we expect to be graded or judged by the way we write something down. Children are graded on their writing ability at school, but when we use writing as a tool for teaching stewardship it is important to allow freedom of expression and not correct grammar or spelling. Even now, as a published author, when the thoughts are flowing. I first write without regard to spelling and grammar and go back later to finish and polish up the text. The exception to this would be a project that will be presented to the whole church. Then the class can work together, with the teacher's guidance, in preparing it for "publication."

Creative writing is not a gift of every person, but it is a means by which everyone can write out his or her thoughts. The writer may never reread what was written, but once it is put on paper the thinking process becomes clearer.

Younger children will need to voice their thoughts for adults to write. Even if they cannot read what is written, they thrill to see their thoughts in writing. Encourage beginning writers to record their thoughts and develop their writing skills.

All children can deal with some sort of research projects. Stewardship research can include ways that the church spends money; needs of people in a mission where you spend money; places the church can recycle its office paper; the amount of water we waste on occasions, such as leaving the water running while brushing teeth; comparison shopping for name brand items versus generic brands. Since most children are familiar with the computer, they will enjoy doing some of the research online.

As you work with children on writing or research assignments, remember that we do not teach grammar and composition in Christian education. Our time is far too precious to spend it on those goals. The school system is responsible for that. We must work with the skills children attain elsewhere. Writing and research are our tools to help children record good ideas and better understand the way they think and feel inside. Assure them that they only need to write in a form they can read themselves and that you will later work together on editing anything that will be published for others to read.

Approach writing assignments in various ways. Too often, we make writing "copy" assignments, giving children certain verses on various themes to copy on paper. This does not create learning. Instead, it creates boredom. Writing assignments need to be creative. They must involve thought about the subject. The learning comes through the experience, and that experience is more pleasurable when done in cooperation with others. Therefore, unless it's a personal reflection experience, I work on writing assignments as a large group or in small groups. Working in groups also helps remove the competitive attitude. Children in any age grouping have a variety of reading and writing levels, and all of them will be better able to participate when they work in groups.

Although the experiences in this chapter primarily deal with elementary children (because of their ability to read and write), preschoolers may participate in some of the research projects that do not require reading, or in which reading can be done by adults. The children then would decide what to include in the "report".

Biblical Research on Stewardship

Children need to realize that the Bible makes frequent references to the importance of stewardship and giving to God. Reproduce page 57 and use it for older children to research some of the biblical references.

Stewardship in the Bible

Look up the following Bible passages and answer the questions after each passage.

GENESIS 1:26

If we were made in the image of God and are to follow God's command here, what must we do about the earth? _____

_____

GENESIS 14:18-20

What amount of his wealth did Abram give to the priest of God? _____

_____

GENESIS 28:20-22

What did Jacob pledge to give to God? _____

LEVITICUS 25:1-5

How does Moses tell the people to be stewards of the land? _____

_____

LEVITICUS 27:30

What did Moses say that the Lord wants?_____

DEUTERONOMY 8:18

What does this passage say about wealth? _____

_____

DEUTERONOMY 14:22

What tithe (one-tenth) is spoken of here? What can that correspond to for today?

_____

PSALM 8:6-8

What has God given us to care for? _____

ACTS 4:32-35

How did the people in the early church share the things they had? _____

_____

1 PETER 4:10

How are we to use the gifts (talents) that God gave us? _____

Documentary: Hometown Stewardship

Today's cameras make it easy for most elementary children to carry out this project. Even preschoolers can work on this with the help of an adult. Move about town, looking for ways that we practice good and poor stewardship in nature. Take photos of the evidence and record the locations. Make a documentary book or video to show your findings. Include some statement about how to change each example of poor stewardship. With digital cameras, this could easily be made into a slide show, or you could use a video recorder and add voices of the children explaining the photos.

Some suggestions of what you may look for include stagnant water, soil erosion, clear cutting for housing, large areas of paving with no trees, littered roadside, junk strewn yards, leaking faucets or constantly running water fountains, and such.

Energy Interviews

Arrange for the children to conduct interviews with adults about the ways they are God's stewards and save energy. The interviews may be video recorded, or written up in book form. This could also be an ongoing project with an interview published each month in your church newsletter. With regular publication, the children help educate the adults about the true meaning of stewardship. Be sure in the interview to speak of saving energy as a way to be God's steward.

Gifts for God

This writing activity might be used during Lent or during your stewardship commitment time. Use fall or spring colors for the construction paper, depending on the time of year.

Discuss with the children the importance of being stewards of our time. God gives us twenty-four hours each day. Eight to ten hours of that is God's gift of rest or sleep, but the remaining fourteen to sixteen hours it is our responsibility to be good stewards.

Give each child several pieces of colorful paper. Ask them to write gifts of time that they can give back to God. These might include service in the church, service to others, caring for some part of God's world, care for their bodies, study of the Bible, study in school to improve their minds, and so on.

Fold each paper in accordion fashion. Lay a pipe cleaner in the middle of the fold and tightly twist the pipe cleaner once around the folded paper. Twist each "gift" around the branch of a tree displayed in the classroom, or on a cross made of small branches.

Close with a prayer, thanking God for the gift of time and dedicating these gifts of time back to God.

Hands of a Steward

This is simple enough for any age child. Draw an outline of each child's hand on paper. Ask the children to think of ways they can be good stewards at home or at school, and write one item on each finger. Cut the hands out, or leave them intact on the paper. Be sure the name of the child is on the paper before sending it home. The hands will remind the children to carry out these acts during the week. Follow up the next week, asking what acts they were able to carry out.

Hunger and Starvation Research

In our well-fed society, we often use the term *starving* to indicate hunger. Most of us actually have no idea just how the starvation process occurs. Assign teams to use encyclopedias and magazines to research the topic and report their findings to the class.

They are likely to find that starvation comes from medically acute malnutrition, a result of not having enough to eat or drink. In order to survive, the body first devours its fat, then its muscle. Muscles no longer cushion bones, hair becomes thin and falls out, skin peels, nails crack, and gums and joints bleed because of vitamin deficiencies. We lose our immunity to disease, and our brain cells die, taking away our ability to reason, even our ability to think of ways to obtain food.

Older children can create family meditations around the information they find and publish them for church members to use during the weeks that your church emphasizes stewardship. Use a daily Bible passage and two or three sentences of information on hunger. This family meditation booklet can also be prepared for the Lenten season.

Hunger Elimination

It is estimated that hunger around the world could be eliminated by 2015 if everyone in the United States gave seven cents a day for hunger. Help students complete the following form for their family. When they have finished, talk together about items they enjoy, but are not necessities, that equal the different answers in the equation.

_____ family members X 7 cents = _____ a day
X 7 days = _____ a week
X 4 weeks = _____ a month
X 12 months = _____ a year
What might your family give up in order to do this?

Inheritance Problem

Children with a basic working knowledge of math can work with this research. Use the following situation problem to talk about how we use our money as God's stewards:

There was a father who had two children. He said, "I want to give you an inheritance. I can give it to you in either of two ways, and you must choose which way you want to receive it.

1. I will give you a million dollars right now, for you to do with as you please.

2. I will give you one cent today, and double it every month for three years.

Which do you choose?

Have the children decide immediately which they would choose. Then have them work the problem and see if they still feel right about the choice.

(Note: The second choice receives the most money. The last month of the first year the person would receive $20.48. The amount that the father would give in the last month of the second year would be $83,886.08. And $343,597,383.68 would be given in the last month of the third year alone. In solving this problem, we can forget that the recipient in the second case receives double each month, but still has what was given in the previous months. By the time you add all of the months together the amount is almost incomprehensible.)

As you debrief, talk about making good use of everything God has given us by planning carefully. Use these passages, along with a discussion on the way we use our money: Matthew 6:24; Luke 12:31-34; and I John 3:17. Help the children realize that we do not want to make money in order to possess it, but rather to be able to use it as God's stewards.

Journaling

Journaling is different from a diary. In a diary you record things that happen each day. A journal may mention happenings in a day, but it is primarily a recording of thoughts that the person has about specific things or about events. Sometimes we journal around events that happen; sometimes about people we meet; sometimes using scripture or writings of other people.

There are no rules for journaling, and it may be done with varying frequency. Consider giving each child a spiral notebook and pencil at the beginning of the year or the beginning of a specific time. Structure your class period so that there are ten minutes for journaling as soon as they arrive in the classroom. Suggest they reflect on their week as they write in their journals. Suggest that they include specific acts of stewardship that they or others have done and how they felt when they accomplished the acts.

Keep the journals in the classroom, assuring the students that they will not be read by you or anyone else. At the end of the year or designated period, send the journals home for them to keep. If at any time students wish to share something that they wrote in their journals, provide the opportunity.

Litter Research

This activity gives the children opportunity to act as stewards of God's creation as they learn a little about litter. Give each child a plastic bag and a plastic glove. Take everyone out on the lawn (or other designated area) and tell them to fill the bags with trash or litter of any kind that they find. Warn the children to be careful when picking up sharp objects. If they will be near traffic, arrange for orange vests or other bright clothing so that they will be easily seen.

After an appointed amount of time, bring everyone together (inside or out) and separate the litter into two piles: "natural" litter (dead leaves, branches, and such) and "people" litter (plastic cups, drink cans, paper, and such). Ask the children to study what they gathered. Use the following questions for discussion. You may also point out some of the information under "Decomposing Timeline" on page 28 if you picked up some of those items.

- Which pile is larger?

- Does any of the litter harm our environment in any way? How?

- How does this litter cause sight pollution (unsightly things we see)?

- If any of the litter harms our environment, how can we reduce the harm it does?

- If it takes 1,000 gallons of water to produce aluminum for one can, how much water did you save by recycling the cans you found?

- Does our church recycle cans used on the church grounds? If not, how can we help this to come about?

Newspaper Research

Search through newspapers for stories of people who have acted as stewards. Create a stewardship bulletin board with these stories and pictures. Place the bulletin board where the whole church family can see it.

OR

Select newspaper stories that (1) tell of persons who were good stewards and (2) tell of persons who were bad stewards. Discuss why more bad news than good news is reported, and how we can help change this.

Poetry

Most of us shy away from creating poetry, but actually, inside all of us, hides a poet's thoughts. Some children will enjoy certain styles of poetry, and others will grasp another style. Experiment with several styles at different times. You may discover that one style is more popular with your children than another. Be aware of new students coming into your class and offer them an opportunity to try different styles.

Never say to children, "Write a poem" about something. Give them direction for one style or another. Below are the four forms I most frequently use:

1. *Picture poems* use words or phrases to outline the shape of a symbol or object. The words may express feelings or thoughts about the subject.

The moon curl up to the sky reaching for its Creator than turns and comes back to the earth reminding us that we are one

2. *Cinquain* (sin-cane) poetry is not as complicated as it sounds, and gives structure to creative thinking. A thesaurus sometimes helps older children, but do not rely on it. The *cinquain* poem has five lines, using this formula:

Line 1: One-word title or subject.

Line 2: Two words that tell about the subject. These words may compose a phrase, or they may be separate words.

Line 3: Three verbs or action words (such as "ing" words), or a three-word phrase about the subject.

Line 4: Four words that tell of the writer's feelings about the subject.

Line 5: The subject word again, or another word that refers back to the title or subject. If the poem is a prayer, this word may be "Amen." *Example:*

Hunger

no   food

pain   dizziness   stumbling

I cannot even think.

Help!

3. *Acrostic* poems use the letters from a word to form the first words of the sentences of a poem. Example:

S ince the beginning, God asked us to care for the earth.

T his is what a steward does:

E lect leaders who care about the earth.

W atch for ways to spend money wisely.

A lways recycle paper, plastic, cans, and glass.

R emind others to be good stewards.

D edicate a tithe (one tenth) of his or her earnings to the Lord.

4. *Free verse* takes various forms. It may include phrases, sentences, or a series of words. The lines may vary in length, and the words may or may not rhyme. Action words give excitement to the poem. Example:

The earth is the Lord's,

the tree, the ocean, the shore.

The earth is the Lord's,

laughing water, screaming wind, and more.
God gave me a charge
    to know, to care, to love.
As steward I work for all,
    on earth and also above.

Product Research

Select a product and use an encyclopedia or search online to learn how a product comes into your home. As an example, bananas go from owner/grower in another country, to picker, to packing company, to shipping company, to importing company, to wholesaler, to retailer, to us. Discuss how good stewards make certain products they buy are produced or manufactured under good working conditions.

    OR

    The following questions reveal how connected we are to people all over the world, and will help your class discuss stewardship.

1. Filament for light from Bolivia. How many lights do you have in your house? _____ **A U.S. child will use 30 to 50 times more goods in a lifetime than one born in Bolivia's poor section.** What did you buy this year that you no longer use? Was that good stewardship? _____

   Why don't you use it anymore? _____

2. Clothing from Costa Rica. How many shirts do you have? _____ **Workers in Costa Rica earn less than 40 cents an hour.** What clothing have you bought simply because it was a new style, not because you needed it?

   _____

   What do you do with the clothing you outgrow? _____

3. Teak furniture from Honduras. What furniture do you have that is made of teak? _____ **About 75 percent of the people in Honduras live in small rural villages and earn about $6.00 a month.** What did you pay for your last toy or computer game? _____

4. Baseball and glove from Haiti. Do you have a baseball and glove? _____ **In a Haitian village of 6,000 people, there usually are only two water taps. One out of every five babies born in Haiti dies before its second birthday.** How many children do you know under the age of two? _____

5. Rubber in sneakers from Thailand. How many pairs of sneakers are there in your house? _____ **Most people in Thailand make $528 a year, or $10.15 a week.** How much allowance do you get a week, and how do you spend it?

   _____

6. Radio assembled in Taiwan. How many radios does your family own? _____ **Workers in Taiwan earn less than 25 cents an hour.** What did you last spend only 25 cents on?

   _____

7. Parts of the television set come from Burundi. How many televisions does your family have? _____ **People in Burundi seldom live to be older than 42 years.** Who do you know who is about 42?

    _____

8. Electricity made from coal mined in Clear Fork Valley, Kentucky. How many electrical outlets are in your house? _____ **Two-thirds of the houses in Clear Fork Valley do not have flush toilets.** How many flush toilets do you have in your house? _____

9. Coffee from Guatemala. Who in your house drinks coffee? _____ **Two out of every three persons in Guatemala make only $42.00 a year.** What have you bought or been given that cost about $42.00? _____

10. Pineapples from the Philippines. Do you eat pineapples or drink the juice? _____ **Half of the children in the Philippines under four years of age are ill because they do not get enough protein.** Who do you know that is under four years of age? _____

11. Cocoa and fish from Ecuador. When do you enjoy cocoa? _____ Do you ever have tuna-fish sandwiches for lunch? _____ **In Ecuador, 60 percent of the children do not have enough to eat to keep them healthy.** What was the longest time you went without food, and how did it feel? _____

12. Sugar from the Dominican Republic. What foods that you like best contain sugar? _____ **Only 30 percent of the children in Dominican Republic ever live to be five years old.** Who do you know that is five? _____

13. Other common items supplied by poor countries: tea from Bangladesh; copper wiring from Chile; aluminum from Jamaica; tin from Malaysia; dog food made of fishmeal from Peru; cork (for bulletin board) from Algeria; natural gas from Mexico.

Research Favorite Possessions

Prepare papers for each child in the following manner (NOTE: Older children may follow the directions to prepare the pages themselves):

1. Beginning at the bottom of the page, turn up 1½ inches of paper four times, leaving a 3-inch area at the top. In that area, write "My Favorite Possessions," and draw a line along the top fold.

2. Unfold one section and draw a line along the top of that fold. Write in that area, "Favorite Possession #1."

3. Unfold the next section and draw a line along the top of that fold. Write in that area, "Favorite Possession #2."

4. Unfold the next section and draw a line along the top of that fold. Write in that area, "Favorite Possession #3."

5. Unfold the last section and draw a line along the last fold line. Write in that area, "Favorite Possession #4."

6. Refold bottom fold (covering up possession #4), and write on reverse side of page that is folded over, "How would I feel if I could not have possession #4?"

7. Refold the next fold (covering up possession #3), and write on reverse side of page that is folded over, "How would I feel if I could not have possession #3?"

8. Refold the next fold (covering up possession #2), and write on reverse side of page that is folded over, "How would I feel if I could not have possession #2?"

9. Refold the last fold (covering up possession #1), and write on reverse side of page that is folded over, "How would I feel if I could not have possession #1?"

10. Open all of the sheets and lay them flat for each child.

Give a sheet to each child. Ask the children to think about all of the things they own personally, and then ask that they decide on their four favorite possessions. Write these in the four sections indicated. When all have finish, ask them to turn up the first fold, covering up possession #4. Ask them to think about losing that possession, and then answer the question on the folded paper. Continue with all four possessions.

Ask the children to turn their folded paper over and answer these questions on the back:

- What makes it possible for me to have these possessions? (Parents, gifts from others, my job, and so on.)

- Why are my parents (or why am I) able to work to have money to buy possessions? (God gave us ability/brains/talents/opportunities.)

- How can I be a good steward of these possessions?

Talk together about their answers.

Scale of Giving

Draw a big scale on a large piece of paper. Give children small papers cut in the shape of weights. On each paper "weight," they write any reasons for giving they may think of. As a group, discuss the different reasons and tape them on the plus or minus side of the scale, depending upon whether you decide it is a Christian's attitude for giving. In your discussion, point out that God loves with a happy heart and God loves with a sad heart. Even if we don't give to others, God continues to love us, but God intends for all people to live together happily, and God's loves with a happy heart when we give. Finish your discussion by reading Matthew 6:1-4.

Some of the reasons for giving may be:

- Give to church because parents tell you to.

- Give to a friend because he or she will give to you.

- Give because you desire to help others.

- Give to someone because you know it will make that person happy.

- Give to a TV ministry because the evangelist cries, and his voice "moves you" and you are sorry for him.

- Give because someone has told you that you will go to hell if you don't give.

- Give so that God will love you.

- Give because you love God.

- Give because you feel privileged to give as a Christian.

- Give because you recognize that all that you have is actually God's.

Signs of Stewardship

Reproduce copies of the towel on page 71. After discussing ways they can be stewards at home and school, send copies of these home with the children. As the children act in the manner of a steward, they fill in the sign of stewardship on the towels, asking someone in their family to sign their statement. (This not only helps the child think of ways to be a steward, but it involves the adults in the home.) Preschool children can participate in this with the help of parents.

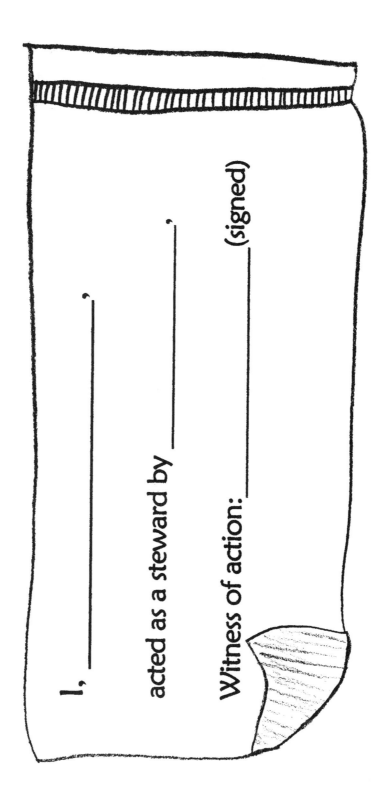

I, _____,

acted as a steward by _____,

Witness of action: _____

(signed)

Stewardship of a Car

Although elementary children are too young to drive, their activities and demands often affect the use of the family automobile. Early development of a good understanding of stewardship in the use of a car will make a difference in their attitudes when they do begin driving. The idea for this activity comes from a curriculum for youth, *The Stewardship of a Car*, by Frankie Garrick, published through the South Caroline United Methodist Conference in 1986.

Divide the class into groups of three to five persons. Give each group a large piece of newsprint and markers, and ask them to fill the newsprint with drawings or words that give reasons for using an automobile. Afterwards, discuss their statements and drawings and discuss which uses are good stewardship and which are simply for pleasure. Discuss how God would have us use our automobiles. (The information in the handout for the mini-retreat on page 107 may help in your discussion.)

Water Research

Young children can research and list the ways we use water each day, then think of ways to be good stewards of water. This can include recycling water in the home, such as watering plants with water they run while waiting for it to get hot.

You might provide a form to ask families to read their water meters daily, then look at the use and discover why they use more water on some days than on others. Discuss ways to cut down on specific water use.

Divide the number of gallons used per day in a family by the number of persons living in the house, and you will know how much is used for each person. Persons in semiarid regions of Africa use only four-fifths of a gallon per day.

Older children can research the way your city recycles water. They can also use encyclopedias, the web, and library books for further information. It might include the following:

- Water covers three-fourths of the earth's surface. Of all our water, 97.4 percent is salt water; 1.8 percent is frozen; and .8 percent is fresh.

- Watering the lawn averages 10 gallons of water per minute. Brushing teeth while leaving the water running can take 10 gallons. By cutting it off while brushing, you can save 9.5 gallons.

- It takes 1,000 gallons of water to produce an aluminum can. Recycling cans will save this water.

- People can live up to two months without food, but will die in three days without water.

- All water is recycled. What you drink today may contain a molecule that a dinosaur once drank.

Worship Expressions

Arrange with the pastor for your class to write some part of the liturgy for Sunday worship. This might be during your stewardship campaign or around earth day, although any Sunday is appropriate, because stewardship should be a lifestyle, and not just for special occasions. Consider one of these:

- a creed about stewardship of time, talents, money, or our environment;

- an offering prayer, thanking God for the gift of money, and dedicating our gifts back to God;

- a poem stressing how people depend upon nature and nature depends upon people;

- paraphrase (see chapter 8) a scripture on stewardship.

Write for Action

Write to businesses, objecting to their advertising or their products. United Methodists in Boston convinced the Converse Shoe Company that "Run 'N Gun" was the wrong name for a sneaker. Although the name comes from a basketball term, with today's use of firearms by children, they convinced the company o change the sneaker name to "Run 'N Slam." Although adults spearheaded this protest, much of the advertising now aims its efforts toward children, recognizing that parents buy what the children want. Therefore, they now listen to the voices of children even more than in the past.

Children can research fast-food restaurants in your community to see which are acting as good stewards by using recyclable products or environment friendly materials. They may write to those who are not, telling them they will ask their parents to use another restaurant unless they switch their practice. Be sure to follow up and if they do switch their practice, use the restaurant, and let them know you appreciate their action.

Another research project asks each child to collect the packaging on everything coming into the house from the store for a week. Measure and weigh the amount of packaging, then write to the companies concerned, telling them of your findings and urging them to reduce their packaging.

Write to government or church officials, with supportive suggestions and informed criticism about their action. When writing, be brief, courteous, and specific about your information or complaint. The letter should be personal and be neatly handwritten or typed. Using form letters is usually a waste of time.

Address Senators: The Honorable _____
                            U.S. Senate
                            Washington, DC 20510

Address Representatives: The Honorable _____
                            U.S. House of Representatives
                            Washington, DC 20515

Chapter Seven:

Games and Puzzle Activities
for Stewardship

BECAUSE THEY INVOLVE MANY LEARNING STYLES, games hold a rung near the top of the learning ladder. They give children opportunities to actually experience situations, and we learn best through experience. We must, however, be cautious about emphasizing the competition that games can bring. We should not use competition as a motivational tool for learning. It is better when we learn for the joy of learning and the excitement of knowledge. Where possible, use games that set goals of everyone finishing the games.

I have tried to include games that do not require expensive equipment or game pieces. By doing this we exhibit good stewardship. Talk with your children about using games that show good stewardship.

Keep on the lookout for appropriate games in your curriculum. When you find one, don't let it go out with the trash at the end of the quarter. Use file folders with envelopes for the game pieces, or find a box for storage. You may laminate the game at a local school or office supply store, at a small cost per foot.

Today's children are taught to play by strict rules and have coaches or game officials who call them when the play is wrong. This eliminates two very good learning opportunities. First, they do not learn to negotiate. Working together to establish the rules of a game teaches children to work with other people. Second, they do not learn to "police" themselves and their own actions. They depend on an outside force and thereby develop the attitude of, "If I'm not caught, then it's ok." As you work with a game, allow the children to help establish part or all the rules. Acknowledge that there may be different ways of playing specific games, since common games sometimes have various sets of rules. Someone in class may say, "We played it this way where I came from." Acknowledge this, and ask if others have played the game in other ways. Try several ways of playing, or several sets of rules, and affirm each one.

Puzzles attract some children, while others find them boring. I never enjoyed them much as a child, but as an adult, I find them challenging. Use puzzles for variety in your activities. Older children will also enjoy creating puzzle games.

Blocks and Rocks

For this you will need to have blocks and some irregular rocks that are about the size of the blocks. On the blocks write (or tape paper with writing on it) ways we can be good stewards. On the rocks, write ways we ignore our stewardship responsibilities. Ask the children to build a structure with the blocks and rocks. As they build, talk about how much firmer the structure is where the blocks are used, mentioning the items written on the blocks. Also talk about how the uneven and irregular rocks can cause the structure to fall down easily. Talk about the items written on the rocks and how they are poor examples of stewardship. After the practice, ask them how the experience of building with blocks and rocks helps us know how to be good stewards.

Here are some examples of items you might put on the blocks and rocks:

Blocks	Rocks
Recycle papers, plastic, glass, and cans	Throw paper, plastic, glass and cans away
Pick up litter	Throw trash on the ground
Give a tithe to the church	Spend all your money on yourself
Volunteer to work on a mission project	Say, "Someone else can do it," when asked to work on a mission project
Turn off water while brushing teeth	Leave water running when brushing teeth
Take short showers	Take long showers

Crossword Stewards

Crossword puzzles are not everyone's favorite activity, but most children who have a good grip of spelling enjoy them. Don't make it a contest to see who can finish first. Let the children work in pairs. After they have worked for a while, work on the puzzle as a group and discuss each of the sentences.

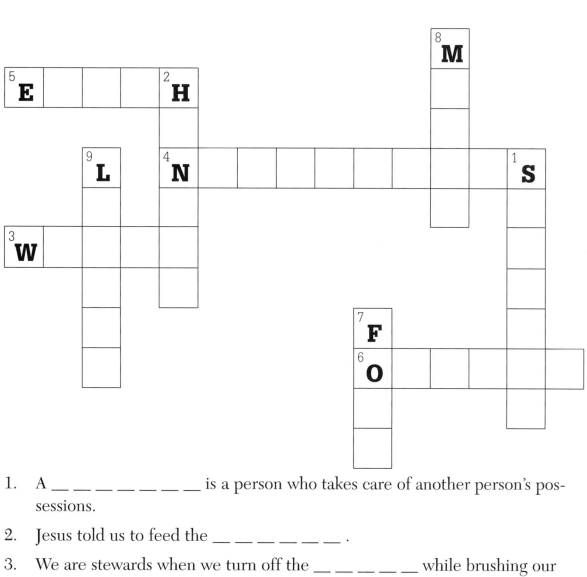

1. A __ __ __ __ __ __ __ is a person who takes care of another person's possessions.

2. Jesus told us to feed the __ __ __ __ __ __ .

3. We are stewards when we turn off the __ __ __ __ __ while brushing our teeth.

4. When stewards recycle __ __ __ __ __ __ __ __ __ __ they save trees.

5. Everything that is in the __ __ __ __ __ __ belongs to God, and we are God's stewards.

6. God gave us talents to make money so that we can care for ourselves and

    __ __ __ __ __ __ .

7. As stewards we collect __ __ __ __ and clothes to share with the homeless.

8. When we give __ __ __ __ __ to our church and the projects of the church, we are stewards.

9. A good steward does not throw __ __ __ __ __ __ on the ground.

Food-Chain Game

Help children learn that, as stewards of the earth, we must recognize and protect the environment and food chains. To prepare for this game, cut out several circles of colorful construction paper. Cut a slit about one-third of the way into each circle. On the circles, write items that make up various food chains. Here are a few, but you can research the library for others:

- acorn/squirrel/fox/bacteria;

- mosquito/dragon fly/frog/turtle/human/bacteria;

- lettuce/worm/robin/bacteria;

- grass/cow/human/bacteria;

- carrots/raccoon/vulture/bacteria.

Mix up the circles and ask the children to take a given number. Then have them move about the room, finding others who have circles that help to make up the food chains. These are then put together.

OR

You may divide the children into groups and hand out a set of circles for each food chain to each group. The children then work with the circles, connecting them in the order of the food chain.

Stewardship Tag

Begin by discussing ways that stewards use their talents to care for others. Tell the children to play with two persons as "it." One person is the tagger, and the other is the steward. When the tagger tags a person, he or she must remain in the same position and not move until the steward comes to give a caring act of stewardship, such as a hug or a pat on the head. Play for a given amount of time, and then exchange and allow others to be the tagger and steward. After the game ask:

- How did you feel while you had to stand still and wait for someone to give you a caring act of stewardship?

- How did you feel after receiving the caring act from the steward, and you were free to move again?

- How did you feel when you acted as a steward and gave the caring act of stewardship?

Chapter Eight:

Music, Rhythm, and Reading Activities for Stewardship

Throughout history, we passed music from generation to generation, in much the same manner as storytelling. Rhythm may even predate music and seems to surge from the heart of our being. Readings combine tone and rhythm. When we celebrate with these methods, we use the gifts that God gave us.

Once children realize they can manipulate their voice tones, they experiment with singing. This does not mean they will always sing on key. In fact, some children sing off key with gusto for years, unless we show them how to listen to a note and move their voices up or down to hit that note. Therefore, do not assume that a child is tone-deaf until you have worked with him or her. You may suggest that children listen to the notes and move their voices appropriately, but I encourage you to leave the actual teaching of music skills to the school and private teachers. Recognize that in Christian education we use music, rhythm, and readings as tools. The experience creates the learning, and we do not aim for performance.

Although some of us feel uncomfortable leading music, we need to include it in our tool chest as we work with children. You might encourage someone else to help you with music in your classroom, or ask someone to help you make audiotapes of songs you want to use. Even if you feel music isn't your gift, I encourage you to experiment with leading, recognizing you are not expected to "perform." Consider this a learning experience for both you and your class.

Children's Choirs

For children, a choir program should be learning-centered, rather than performance-centered. Encourage directors of your choir program to look for opportunities to expand the children's understanding of stewardship through the songs they sing. If the directors emphasize the meaning of the words, music becomes a learning experience.

Choral Reading

Choral reading is done antiphonally (first one group or individual, then another). Be sure to talk with the children about the meaning of the words and how it relates to stewardship.

If you do not want to create your own, you may use poems, scripture, or hymn verses to create a choral reading with a stewardship theme. Look for pieces with phrases that sound both heavy and light. As you work with this, plan for the deeper voices or the whole group to speak the phrases that lend the heavier, or darker, feelings. Lighter phrases may be spoken by higher voices. This example is a paraphrase of Psalm 8:1, 3-9:

> Leader: O Lord, our Sovereign,
>
> **Group: how majestic is your name in all the earth!**
>
> Solo 1: You have set your glory above the heavens.
>
> Solo 2: When I look at your heavens, the work of your fingers, the moon and the stars that you established;
>
> Solo 3: what are human beings that you are mindful of them, mortals that you care for them?
>
> **Group: Yet you have made them a little lower than God, and crowned them with glory and honor.**
>
> Solo 1: You have given them dominion over the works of your hands;
>
> Solo 2: you have put all things under their feet, all sheep and oxen,
>
> Solo 1: and also the beasts of the field, the birds of the air, and the fish of the sea.
>
> Solo 2: Whatever passes along the paths of the sea.
>
> **Group: O Lord, our Sovereign, how majestic is your name in all the earth!**

Creating Songs or Hymns

By creating songs and hymns, children think about ways they can be stewards for God. You might use some of the creation verses or scriptures mentioned in the first chapters of this book as a basis for your songs. Or you could make up phrases about stewardship and follow these steps to create songs or hymns:

1. Take one phrase at a time. Read or say it together for the "pulse" or rhythm. Change the wording slightly until you agree on the right rhythm but keep the original meaning.

2. Ask several students to speak the phrase using the same rhythm. Listen to how some speak high, and some speak low. Refer to this as "color" sounds. Affirm any uniqueness.

3. Listen again to the rise and fall of the voices and ask if any student will try to duplicate it with music. You may need to give a tone. Use the key of C and play C, E, G.

4. Sing the phrase several times, using the student's tune.

5. Move to other phrases, periodically repeating the whole song. (Adapted from Delia Halverson, *How to Train Volunteer Teachers* [Nashville: Abingdon Press, 1991], Handout 19.)

Accept the children's tunes, remembering that you are not working to create professional songwriters; instead you are using the experience for learning about stewardship.

You may also use familiar tunes for your songs, such as: "Oats, Peas, Beans, and Barley Grow," "The Farmer in the Dell," "Twinkle, Twinkle, Little Star." Try these lines to the tune of "Are You Sleeping, Brother John?"

Serving God; serving God.
This we do. This we do.
We are all God's stewards.
We are all God's stewards.
You and me. You and me.

Sing this next song to the tune of the hymn "A Charge to Keep I Have."

A Charge to Care

A charge to care I have,
A God to glorify,
Care for the world and all of life
On earth and in the sky.

A steward of the earth,
Plants, water, creatures, trees.
My goal in life, my joy and love:
My Lord and God to please.

I hear God's charge again,
"See that my earth is kept."
Yes, Lord, I pledge my life to you,
Your trust, I now accept. Amen.

(From Delia Halverson, *New Call to Mission*, student book [Nashville: Graded Press, 1990], p. 8.)

Heritage Readings

Search the library for books of poems and readings. Using these not only helps children learn about stewardship, but it also lifts up our heritage of leaders in past generations. We recognize that people through the ages have acted as stewards and cared for the world and God's people.

Prayer of Saint Francis Assisi

Lord, make me an instrument of thy peace.
Where there is hatred, let me sow love;
Where there is injury, pardon;
Where there is doubt, faith;
Where there is despair, hope;
Where there is darkness, light;
Where there is sadness, joy.
O divine Master, grant that I may not so much seek
To be consoled, as to console;
To be understood, as to understand;
To be loved, as to love; for
It is in giving, that we receive;
It is in pardoning, that we are pardoned;
And it is in dying, that we are born to eternal life.

          Amen.

Using the thoughts in Saint Francis' prayer, lead your class in the following litany. Before using the litany, talk about how stewardship involves giving because God gives to us. We give to the world, give to other people, and give to God. Discuss how stewards of God live together in harmony with the earth and with each other.

Group: Lord, make us instruments of your peace.
Voice 1: Where there is hatred,
Group: Let us give love;
Voice 2: Where there is injury,
Group: Let us pardon;
Voice 3: Where there is doubt,
Group: Let us give faith;
Voice 4: Where there is despair,
Group: Let us give hope;
Voice 5: Where there is darkness,
Group: Let us bring light;
Voice 6: Where there is sadness,
Group: Let us spread joy;
Leader: As we follow these ways, we will follow Christ. By following Christ, we bring closer the time when all the world will say:
Group: "We live in harmony together, as God made us to live!" Amen.

Hymns and Songs

Look through your hymnal for hymns that carry the theme of our responsibility to God and to all of God's creation, including people. You may find these in the topical index under such subjects as earth, love, missions, nature, outreach, peace, and stewardship.

Young children enjoy the song, "We Are the Church Together." This song emphasizes the church as inclusive of *all* who worship Jesus, all around the world. We can use it to emphasize our stewardship responsibility to all people.

Be alert to popular songs that carry the theme of caring for the earth. Consider unique ways to adapt the songs to your use. For example, sing "He's Got the Whole World in His Hands," using "bright, pretty flowers" or "animals in the woods" or "all birds that fly." (Note: I prefer to change the wording of this song to: "The whole world is in God's hands.")

Rhythm and Rap

Your children may be more experienced in developing rhythm or rap than you. Encourage them to work with you on the creation. Crating an expression of rhythm and rap may begin with the words, or with the rhythm. It is usually easiest to come up with one phrase and repeat it from time to time throughout the rap. Clap out the rhythm and listen to the phrase. You may need to change it in order to come up with an easy rhythm.

You might also check the hymnal for rhythms in familiar hymns, then work to fit words into that rhythm. Remember that this rap or rhythm is spoken without music. Here is an example, using Matthew 25:31-46. Accent the words or syllables underlined. If you use this, remind the children that, as stewards for God, we must care for other people.

Solo: As <u>to</u> the <u>least</u> of <u>these</u> you <u>did</u>, you <u>al</u>-so <u>did</u> to <u>me</u>.
Group: But <u>when</u> did we <u>see</u> you <u>hun</u>-gry, <u>Lord</u>?
   And <u>when</u> did we <u>see</u> you in <u>pain</u>?
Solo: As <u>to</u> the <u>least</u> of <u>these</u> you <u>did</u>, you <u>al</u>-so <u>did</u> to <u>me</u>.
Group: We <u>al</u>-ways <u>wel</u>-comed <u>you</u> with <u>joy</u>.
   We <u>don't</u> re-<u>call</u> you in <u>need</u>.
Solo: As <u>to</u> the <u>least</u> of <u>these</u> you <u>did</u>, you <u>al</u>-so <u>did</u> to <u>me</u>.
Group: You are <u>right</u>, our Lord, <u>we</u> were blind.
   For-<u>give</u> us, we <u>un</u>-der-<u>stand</u>,
   As <u>to</u> the <u>least</u> of <u>these</u> we <u>did</u>, we <u>al</u>-so <u>did</u> to <u>you</u>.

Litany

In a litany, the whole group responds with a word or phrase after one or more lines. It may be a statement or creed, or it may be a prayer. Everyone may say the words of the litany at once, or the sentences may be divided and read by different parts of the group.

You may want to set up the framework for a litany (such as the one below) and then have your class, or individuals in your class, complete it.

Stewardship of Time

All: Our God, you have given us the gift of time.
Voice 1: We can use time to be _____,
Voice 2: and time to do _____.
Voice 3: We can use time to help _____,

Voice 4: and time to think about _____.

All: We don't always remember that you gave us the gift of time.

Voice 5: We sometimes waste our time by _____,

Voice 6: or we _____ instead of _____.

All: Forgive us, O God. We realize that we are stewards of our time.

Voice 7: Help us use our time _____.

Voice 8: Show us how to _____.

All: We will try to remember to be good stewards of our time. Amen.

Paraphrase

When we paraphrase, we put the scripture or other writing into our own words, rather than those of the author, but retain the real meaning. Paraphrases may be set to music or rhythm, or used as readings by the group or by individuals.

After several opportunities of paraphrasing as a class, older children can locate a scripture and work independently or in small groups on paraphrasing. Young children need shorter verses and require more help. Matthew 6:21 and Luke 12:34 might be paraphrased: *People will know what is important to you when they see what you spend your money on.*

With older children, you might try paraphrasing in the reverse concept. If you do this, be certain the children understand that your purpose is to stimulate thought, and always compare the paraphrase with the actual scripture.

Compare the following negative paraphrase of the Lord's Prayer to the words that Jesus gave us. Talk about which words in the paraphrase are selfish. Discuss the way Jesus used words that showed us how to be a good steward and care for others.

A Selfish Paraphrase of the Lord's Prayer

My Father, who provides for me. Hallowed by thy name. Thy kingdom come, thy will be done, if it doesn't inconvenience me here on earth. Give me today ten times the amount I need. I will use it today and ask for more tomorrow. Forgive me, but take away the consequences. Don't worry about the others, for they surely caused their own problems! Lead me away from knowledge of how others are suffering. Let my eyes see no hard times that come to others. For you are powerful and can make me great! Forever! Amen.

Talent Song

Ask each person to think of one thing that he or she does well. Each time a child shares the talent with the group, sing a verse affirming that talent, using the tune to "Have You Ever Seen a Lassie?" Example:

> Mari-lyn trains the dogs,
>> the dogs, the dogs,
> Mari-lyn trains the dogs,
>> We all give God thanks.
>
> Ruthe-ford knows his ma-th,
>> His ma-th, his ma-th,
> Ruthe-ford knows his ma-th.
>> We all give God thanks.

Chapter Nine:

Celebrations, Projects, and Hands-on Experiences for Stewardship

NO ONE PAYS ATTENTION TO US KIDS! They say, 'What do you know? You're only children.'"

We adults are often guilty of such a statement, or we may have that attitude even if we don't say it out loud. A group of fifth-graders in Saint Paul United Methodist Church in Atlanta did not let that attitude from adults stop them, and they did make a difference.

Class time was over, and the weary teachers weren't really sure the children had grasped the central thought of the morning. They had talked about our responsibility as stewards to care for the earth. As the children spilled out the doors, they headed for the fellowship hall and the refreshments shared by all ages between Sunday school and church. After a brief conversation concerning the morning, the teachers followed.

At the door to the fellowship hall, the teachers ran head-on into most of the fifth-graders, rushing out the door with Styrofoam cups in hand. They approached the teachers with questions:

"Why do we use Styrofoam cups at church? Shouldn't we be better stewards of our world?"

The teachers suggested that they talk with their parents during the week, and a couple of children were assigned to check with the church office about why they used Styrofoam cups. They would all discuss it the next Sunday.

The class discovered that the church had no specific policy for types of cups, just that they'd always used this kind. During the next week, class members worked with the Children's Council to find a better way. They made calls to suppliers and discovered that Styrofoam cups cost one cent each, while paper hot-drink cups cost eight cents each. The class members knew that they must organize a good presentation to convince the church to switch. Another option was to use cups that could be washed and reused.

The children and adults spent several days preparing their presentation, collecting information about the pros and cons of Styrofoam cups and the importance of the other options. They based their suggestions on the biblical concept of stewardship. As a result, the whole church's attitude was turned around! Now the church uses glasses and cups and washes them after each use. It can be done, and children can do it!

Adopt-a-Family

Look for opportunities to pair up families from your church with families from other churches, or families that you contact through other non-profit organizations. Stress this as a way we act as stewards, caring for God's people.

With the hurricane devastations there are families who have lost so much. Some of the common losses will have occurred in areas where children can be involved. Some may have lost Christmas decorations, or books and computer games. Contact your denomination or other church networking organizations to set this up.

The families in one church in Florida made duplicate Advent wreaths, keeping one for themselves and sending the others to their adopted families. They also developed an Advent devotional booklet to go along with the wreaths, so that families in both churches could use the same devotions during the season.

Bike or Hike Sunday

On a given Sunday, encourage everyone to bike or hike to church in order to saving gas and air pollution. On that Sunday, pin a badge on each person who biked or hiked, stating the miles traveled. Calculate the number of miles, and recognize the people and the total number of miles during the worship service. You might also calculate the amount of fuel saved.

If all your members live a great distance from the church, an alternative is a Carpool Sunday. During the service, recognize the families that carpooled to church and the amount of fuel saved. This experience also helps families recognize that they live in the same neighborhood.

Birthday Celebration for Stewards

This can be either an individual or a group project. It will help children recognize that we must be stewards when we purchase (or ask for) toys for our birthdays. Encourage children to ask that food or clothing, instead of toys, be brought to their birthday parties. Then plan a trip to a local mission to deliver the food and clothing. Or you may arrange ahead of time for a special mission to receive the food and clothing and find out the sizes of the clothing needed.

OR

Plan a birthday for Jesus celebration. This may be a part of a children's choir program during Advent, or just a mid-summer celebration. During the event, children (and adults) bring a gift (money or predetermined articles) to the front when their birthday month is called. Stress the fact that we are God's stewards when we care for others.

You might include a birthday cake with twelve candles and light one candle for each month as it is called. Everyone can enjoy the birthday cake afterwards.

Calendar for Stewardship

Create a calendar for the month. As a class, decide on specific thoughts or actions about stewardship and print them on each day. Print the calendar and distribute it to families in the church. (See chapter six for ideas.)

Care Packages

Living a stewardship lifestyle, children can learn to share with those in need. Besides the usual packages for mission agencies, consider persons in your own congregation who are away from home, such as college students or persons in the armed services. Include such items as:

- church bulletins/newsletters;

- devotional items;

- fast-food restaurant coupons;

- home-baked goods;

- microwave popcorn;

- notes from the congregation written earlier on 3 x 5 cards;

- photos of church activities;

- sermon tapes;

- small banners with fun thoughts.

Involve the entire congregational by purchasing the items ahead and displaying them on tables after a worship service. Then ask members to "buy" items to include in the packages. Have the boxes ready for packing, and when an item is "purchased," the purchaser can place the item in the box.

Celebrate God's World

On an appointed Sunday, invite everyone in the church to bring from home a potted plant, a vase of flowers or weeds, or a branch of a tree. Use them to decorate the front of the sanctuary. Use scripture and songs that point out the beauty of God's creation and our responsibility as stewards (Leviticus 25; Deuteronomy 8, 15, and 26; Psalm 8:6-8; 24:1; 50:10-11, 12b).

Celebration of Stewardship Service

Plan an intergenerational celebration to point out the many ways we are stewards throughout the community, not just in the church. This emphasizes a lifestyle of stewardship throughout the week and throughout the community.

This may be done during a worship service or as a church-wide special celebration event, perhaps including a meal and an intergenerational stewardship study.

Ask each church member to list the various ways that they volunteer their time as stewards in the community and in the church. List these in the bulletin or on a large poster. You may use the scripture in Matthew 25:31-46 or John 13:1-20. If you refer to the passage from John, use a towel and basin as symbols for the celebration. Make the occasion festive with balloons and streamers, and recognize how each person is a steward for God.

Community Project

Children can care for God's earth and people within their own community. Consider ways to care for the earth and for people in need. Clean up a vacant lot, plant trees, adopt a stream or road, or volunteer in an agency that helps homeless or abused children. Some churches set aside a specific day and call it "The Great Day of Service".

The churches plan community projects that all ages can participate in, and everyone meets at the church for breakfast and a sending forth service before they begin.

Compost

Make a living example of stewardship and care for the earth by establishing a compost box on church property for the entire congregation to use. Work grass clippings, kitchen discards, and so on into the dirt. You might even rent or purchase a chipper for large items. When the soil is ready, church members may come and take dirt for home use. Contact your local County Extension Agent or www.compostguide.com for information on setting it up.

Environment Friendly Displays

Canvass local businesses and check in local stores to find companies that practice environmentally friendly policies. Prepare a display on a bulletin board or table with products in recyclable or refillable packaging. You might also print up a "Stewardship Yellow Pages" with these businesses.

Or gather information on companies that protect the environment, improve safety and morale conditions for employees, and help urban and community situations. Contact the advocacy group called Businesses for Social Responsibility for information on such companies. Most states have their own organization, or contact the national organization at www.bsr.org.

Field Trips

Plan a field trip that focuses on a specific tree, plot of ground, city block, or creek. Or you might visit parks, museums, parades, or ride on public transportation. Observe, observe, observe! Record (in writing or on tape) everything you see and hear. This might include good and poor conditions of nature and living conditions of people. Afterward, talk about what you have seen and whether the conditions indicate good stewardship or not. Consider ways you might help to change the poor conditions.

Garden of Stewardship

Use a section of the church property to demonstrate a garden where good stewardship is put into practice. This would include eco-friendly fertilizer, compost materials, etc. When the garden produces, collect the food and give it to a soup kitchen, use it for your church suppers, or sell the vegetables to church members and use the money for missions.

Joyful Giving

All giving is an act of stewardship. Most churches have some sort of collection for the needy, but it usually becomes a routine procedure. Spice it up by designing a way to involve the whole church. Your class can sponsor it and advertise it throughout the church. Locate agencies ahead of time to determine specific needs. Divide the needs into groupings appropriate to ages and distribute the lists in a creative way.

Some churches hand out "Bountiful Bags" in graduated sizes according to the needs, with the lists of needs attached. (They use grocery bags that have been decorated.) Others ask that the items be brought in shoeboxes. One church provided giant stockings to fill during Advent.

Be creative with collection points. No one gets excited about dropping a can of soup in a plain cardboard box! Locate some "basement carpenters" who can make slatted wooden boxes for collection. Or decorate baskets and place them at strategic places around the church. You might set aside a specific Sunday and ask that the gifts be brought to the front of the church, as each family enters for worship. Plan a "Food Shower" in the spring and decorate the boxes with umbrellas. At Thanksgiving, create a huge basket or cornucopia for the collection; at Christmas, provide a specific tree under which the items are to be deposited. Celebrate, and make giving a joy!

Mission Trip Celebration

Many churches now plan mission trips for youth and adults. Involve children in dedication services before people leave on a mission, and celebrations upon their return. If the dedication service is during a worship time, plan it for the time of the children's message or before any children leave the worship area. If there are children elsewhere during that time, bring them into the worship area to experience the dedication service. Emphasize the fact that the people going on the mission trip are acting as stewards for God's world and God's people. Ask the children to pray for the mission.

Consider giving small towels to those participating in the celebration, or to those involved with the mission. Decorate the towels with some symbol typical of the mission, along with the dates of the trip. Have children decorate the towels as their part of the celebration. Explain the towel and basin as a symbol of service, using John 13:1-20.

You may also plan a celebration when professional missionaries come to visit. Children need to recognize these people as stewards for God, but also to see them as ordinary people who follow God's call to be stewards at other places than their own communities.

New from Old

Bring discarded items to the church. On a specific day, come together as families and individuals to recycle the items by making something out of them. Some examples might be stuffed toys from old jeans, scrap paper holders, pencil holders, vases, plant holders, and such. Remind the participants that stewards work to recycle items instead of buying new ones.

Newspaper Forest

Ask everyone in the church to bring old newspapers one Sunday. As they drop the newspapers off at a visible location, have children on hand to stack the papers in four-foot-high piles. For each four-foot stack, one large tree had to be cut. You might even make large leaves out of recycled green construction paper to decorate each stack. When all newspapers are collected, count the number of "trees" and report this to the congregation. Point out the importance of recycling newspapers in order to be good stewards of God's earth. Write up a report for your newsletter or ask a local newspaper reporter to cover the event and write about the importance or recycling newspapers.

If your community does not collect newspapers at the curb, help the children spearhead a project of having a recycle bin placed on your property and advertising it in your community.

Plant Trees

Tree planting can be as large or as small a project as you like. Help the children understand that trees make a difference in our environment. We need trees and other plants that make oxygen so that we can breath.

Write a litany to be used in worship in connection with this project. You might use Genesis 1:11-12, 29-30, or Psalm 1:3 as a basis for the litany. Visit these web sights for more information: TreePeople (www.TreePeople.org); National Arbor Day Foundation (www.arborday.org)

To plant a mini-forest, you might find a farmer or landowner in your church or community willing to donate the use of land for tree planting. To obtain trees at little or no cost, call your local United States Department of Agriculture Soil Conservation Office, your local County Cooperative Extension Service, or the National Arbor Day Foundation.

What an example of stewardship a church could give by purchasing some property and beginning a *Confirmation Forest*. Each confirmation class could plant additional trees, and care for the forest would be an ongoing project for each year's class, throughout their study year. (See the story below about Roger Beumeister.)

Arrange with your grounds committee or trustees to plant a tree at church. This can be a project for children of any age, with the help of adults. The tree can be in honor or in memory of someone. You might involve parents in the planning and preparation for this project, and encourage families to plant trees in their own yards.

Plant a gift tree to acknowledge a marriage, anniversary, the birth, baptism, or confirmation of a child, or some other special event. Contact a local nursery about special prices.

Roger Baumeister

The Missouri State Park Board began a project of reclaiming thousands of acres of stripped land for future recreational parks because of one man.

Over thirty years ago Roger Baumeister had a dream for something better for forty-two acres of land that had been stripped by mining and left ugly, eroding, and void of growth. He set about changing the area by hand-planting 75,000 evergreen seedlings and shrubs. These he got at a nominal fee through a state program. The six-acre pit, left from a mining endeavor, is now a six-acre lake full of fish and nesting waterfowl. The forest of new trees attracts rabbits, foxes, deer, quail, and even coyotes and has many hiking trails.

Recycled Care Bears and Quilts

By using old blue jeans or other old clothing that is in good condition, the whole church can work on a project that teaches children to recycle. Locate a simple pattern and, using the old clothing, make teddy bears (or other stuffed toys) or pillows for hospitals, nursing homes, and shelters for abused or homeless persons. Adult classes or women's groups might sew the toys or pillows, and the children could stuff them. The older children can help cut the fabric.

Use recycled clothing for making quilts as well. Younger children can make cards to accompany the quilts. Include a statement in the card that says that this is a way of being a good steward. Older children can cut the squares and tie the quilts. Children of all ages and adults can decorate quilt squares of light solid colors with fabric paints or fabric crayons.

Plan opportunities for the children and adults to work together, or at least plan some activity together, such as delivering the gifts. Children's experiences with older adults are as important as their experience in living stewardship.

Recycle Shop

Recycling is a definite act of stewardship. This can be a small group or even a church wide experience. You can plan it for a specific item (such as a book or record) or for all household items. The rule of thumb is that everyone who brings an item may take something home. Or items can be bought for a nominal price. The object is not to raise money, but to encourage the act of recycling instead of purchasing new. Any money raised through the Recycle Shop can go to a mission.

Or you might simply come together as families and barter to exchange items. This takes less organization, and also results in verbal exchange between families. Insist that everyone recognize this as a way to act as good stewards by sharing items no longer wanted.

Stewardship Coupons

Make Stewardship Coupons similar to the example below and hand them out to the congregation.

Stewardship Coupon

I, _____

will make stewardship my lifestyle by _____

_____

Signed _____

Staple them together in groups of five and encourage individuals to fill them out and give them to others. Talk with your pastor about making this project a part of a Sunday worship which centers on understanding the true meaning of stewardship. Place information about the coupons in the bulletin and newsletter.

Stewardship in Creed/Mission Statement

With older children, go through the creed that your church uses in your worship service, or your church's mission statement. Talk about how a stewardship lifestyle relates to the creed or mission statement. Plan projects or personal deeds to carry out the stewardship in the creeds and mission statements.

Stewardship of Talents

Youth programs often plan opportunities for church members to use the services of teens in order to raise money for a mission project. Why not set up this same opportunity for children? Here are some suggestions. You may come up with better ideas.

Auction of Talents: Set aside a time after worship or during a church dinner and have an auctioneer accept bids for services that children can provide. Another name for this auction might be "Muscles for Missions." Avoid using the term "slave auction," so as not to imply sale of a person.

Barter for Talents: The old art of bartering represents good stewardship. Exchange talents with others, agreeing to do a job or produce a product, in exchange for someone else's talent or product. This may be done at a church gathering or carried out through a bulletin board. Children and families can participate.

Create "Wanted" Posters: Create a poster for each child, including a photo and a description of a job the child will do for money to be given to a mission project. Post the notices around the church building. Be sure to include a space on each poster for adults to sign up for the child's services.

Service Bureau: Set up a grass cutting, pet care, or mail collecting service for families who travel to use while they are away. Select a person to receive the calls and assign each project to a specific child. Help the children recognize that the time they spend on the project is their stewardship gift to God. God gave us twenty-four hours a day, and as good stewards we should use it wisely.

Visual Stewardship

Since giving is an act of stewardship, we must involve children. All projects cannot have on-site experiences. However, all of them can be visually appealing and involve active learning. A congregation in Tucson, Arizona chose three exciting ways to promote its projects. When the children raised money for their Heifer Project, they made "chicks" of yellow pompoms and glued on black paper eyes and an orange paper beak. These were put into plastic Easter eggs. Two nests were made of wood shavings, and the plastic eggs were placed in one nest. Each week the children put their offerings into a hen-shaped basket, and when enough money was collected for one chick, a child opened an egg and placed the "hatched" chick in the second nest.

When they raised money for an infant nutrition program, they used a clear baby bottle to collect the money. They posted pictures of babies, and a mother brought a baby to the classes for a visit.

A construction project that needed tools came to life with a house made of poster board, with small windows and doors that opened. Brown paper "boarded up" the windows and doors, with a price printed on each. When they raised enough funds, they opened the corresponding door or window to reveal the type of tool that the amount of money would purchase.

Other churches often use the idea of collecting pennies by the foot. Seventeen pennies make a foot. Calculate how many feet of pennies you will need for a specific project, and work toward that goal. Make the stewardship act of giving exciting!

A church in Georgia collected money for tricycles and gave them to children who needed them. They made a large drawing of the parts of a tricycle (wheels, handle bars, seat, etc.), and as they raised a given amount of money, they added a part.

During Vacation Bible School a Florida church purchased school supplies for a nearby mission. After each offering, supplies were actually purchased and placed at the front of the sanctuary where they gathered. The children watched the mound of school supplies grow, and just before the beginning of school, several children went with adults to deliver the supplies to the mission.

Be creative in your promotion of a project! Ask the children to help you think of new and different ways to display your project.

Worship with the Homeless

Children need to recognize that we are stewards when we care for the homeless. It is important that they realize homeless people are as important to God as each of us.

Homeless people seldom feel comfortable attending a worship service where everyone dresses up. Some congregations, in areas where homeless people live, now plan informal worship services where they will be more comfortable. Check your community for such services, or plan to establish one through your church.

Church Street United Methodist Church in Knoxville, Tennessee established such a dress-down service on Thursday nights. College professors, third-generation homeless persons, children with thrift-store shoes, and a bishop's wife worshiped together.

Yard Sale

Consider sponsoring a yard sale, with the proceeds going to a specific mission project. Ask the children to bring toys, books, and clothing to sell. Involve the whole church in the project. Emphasize stewardship of their talents as they prepare for and work in the yard sale; of their possessions as they recycle items for others to use; and of the money they earn for the project. If the project is for your own church, consider tithing one-tenth of what you raise for some project outside the church. Remind the children that selling the items at a reasonable price allows those who cannot afford them to purchase the items. This is also a form of mission.

Chapter Ten:

Involving Children in the Church Stewardship Plan

RALPH WALDO EMERSON is credited as saying, "All children have at least one thing in common. They close their ears to advice but open their eyes to example." As a member of a church council, stewardship committee, or children's council we can be certain that our actions are setting an example for stewardship. By making decisions that model stewardship, we exhibit a role model for the children to follow. The church in Atlanta was not acting in a manner that exhibited stewardship until the sixth grade class called attention to the fact that they were using throw-away cups that did not decompose. The children in the class continued to bring the stewardship lifestyle before the congregation until the church council evaluated the situation and came up with alternatives.

Perhaps the first step for involving children in any stewardship plan is to educate the church leadership in the lifestyle of stewardship so that we are living examples of stewards. If we truly believe that all we have is a free unmerited gift from God, then we will exhibit stewardship through our leadership in the church. We usually think of a steward as being one person. However, any decision-making body of the church sets the example of stewardship. As a steward, the committees and councils will consider God's direction in all that we do. This will include decisions for the use of the congregation's financial resources, the investment of time and energy of both its members and the volunteers in the congregation's ministry, and the care that we take for the property that God has put in our keeping (including our buildings, equipment, vehicles, and such, as well as the general earth environment in which we live).

To do this, the decision-making groups must have a prayerful attitude about all decisions. Charles M. Olsen, in his book, *Transforming Church Boards into Communities of Spiritual Leaders*, suggests that we pattern our church meetings after a worship service. To do this I make up a written agenda that includes praise (a hymn

---

Why Should Children Learn of Stewardship?

You may have questions as to why we should teach stewardship to children. These questions usually come from people who view stewardship as a means for raising the budget. Here are reasons you can give them:

- In today's world children develop a sense of entitlement and dissatisfaction because of the materialistic messages that surround them. They can learn the difference between wants and needs and develop an attitude of gratitude.

- The understanding that God loves us just the way we are and has given us all the gifts we need to share with others combats the commercial world's message that we must buy, buy, buy in order to be accepted.

- The ages between six and ten are the formidable years for development of attitudes of sharing. If sharing does not become their lifestyle, then they develop an attitude that, "The world owes me . . . " Instead, stewardship can teach them that we are blessed and happy to share our blessings.

- For those who tell you that children have no money for stewardship, remind them that the average child today under the age of thirteen has $230 a year in disposable income. Over 500 million heads of households throughout the world have less money than that to spend on feeding and caring for their families.

- Stewardship is about more than money. Children can share their time and talents as well.

or a reading), telling the story (where committee members see God working in self/church), offering (items to be planned, reviewed – what is commonly called the agenda), and sending forth (how/when we will carry out our offering to God). When I first use such a pattern in a church meeting it takes a little longer, but soon the "offering" part of the meeting (planning and decision making) is simplified, because we enter it with a worshipful attitude and God works through each of us. (See sample agenda on pages 103-104 of *Nuts & Bolts of Christian Education*, Delia Halverson.)

Why Involve Children?

I am fortunate to live in the same community as two of my four grandchildren. These twin girls have been a part of our church from the time they were adopted at four days of age. When they were infants we took them into the sanctuary for the worship service each Sunday. I watched their eyes light up when they saw the overhead lights. I saw their happy responses to the caregivers in the nursery during Sunday school. I watch them now, at thirty months of age, as they run down the sidewalk to the church patio and smile and give "high fives" to the adults who greet them. No wonder they say, "I *love* the church!" The church is their extended family, and the church treats them in a manner that respects them as individuals.

Children will recognize that something special is going on during a stewardship campaign. If we don't involve them they will see themselves as outsiders. You can do something as simple as asking children to draw pictures of what they like best about the church. Mount their drawings on a tag board that has your stewardship campaign theme printed on it. Or, you can involve children in a month long study during the time that the adults study. Making reference to the children or to something that children enjoy during a stewardship sermon also embraces the child. It can be as simple as saying, "You children know what it's like to be hungry! When we give to our church we can help hungry people have something to eat." An occasional reference to something they understand draws them into the sermon and makes them feel included.

There is a window of time when preschools and younger elementary children enjoy doing things that adults do. Set a pattern of stewardship during those years and it will follow them through their lives.

There are opportunities during worship when children, as well as adults, can grow in understanding stewardship. The offering time in most churches has become a simple task of passing the plate. Such nonchalance has nothing to do with stewardship. In the true meaning of an offering, we are giving back to God some of what God has trusted to us and even giving our very lives. It should be the act of the people—the act of offering ourselves to God. Many of the African churches participate in the offering with congregational singing as each person brings his or her offering to the front, placing it before God. They sometimes even dance their offering to the front. If children leave for part of the service at your church, plan to take the offering before they leave. If they never participate in the offering during a worship service, they cannot come to a full understanding that the offering is a time we give back to God part of what God has given to us. It is also good to have children help receive the offering. Older children can do it with very little guidance. Younger children (even small preschoolers) can stand with a parent as he or she takes up the offering. When children see someone their age taking part in this act of worship, all children feel included.

You may also plan some specific opportunities for the children to share what they have learned in their stewardship study. Consider helping the children make the "Stewardship Cookies" on page 22 and give them out at church. Place their art so that the whole congregation can view it. This shows the children that we think their ideas are important, and it also makes the adults aware of the children and their spiritual growth.

Involving children during their formative years sets a pattern in their lives and lays a foundation for their personal acceptance of Christ, leading to their confirmation or personal decision to be a part of the church. One of the best ways to do this is to establish stewardship centers in each classroom (see page 19). This will help them experience and recognize the times they give their prayers, their presence, their gifts, and their service.

Steps in Putting Together a Plan for Children

You can find many so-called "Stewardship Plans" (sometimes called capital campaigns) on the Internet, in Christian bookstores, and through denominational boards. As you review them, be certain that the plan goes beyond raising money. There is an old proverb that says you can give a person a fish and feed that person for a day, or you can teach the person to fish and feed the person for a lifetime. We can embark on a "Stewardship Plan" for raising money each year, struggling over how to make it different and more exciting than last year, or we can set up a plan for educating the congregation (children included) in the joyful lifestyle of stewardship and build on it each year.

You may find that the stewardship plans you review do not have a component for children. These steps will help you develop your own plan.

1. In selecting your committee, make certain you have people who understand the learning needs of children, or at least who are interested in learning about those needs and applying them to the plan.

2. Include children in the planning process by asking them to explain what they know about a steward and stewardship. Explain the definition briefly and tell them you are planning a way for them to understand this better. If you have some older elementary children who

Using Envelopes with Children

If your church uses envelopes for giving, be sure to include children in this practice. Here are some suggestions for successfully using envelopes with children.

- Mail the envelopes to the children with information for the parents. You might develop a flyer or brochure with suggestions for the parents as they teach stewardship. Children enjoy receiving mail, and by mailing the envelopes will not get lost before they leave the church building.

- Encourage children to also share gifts of talents and time. This might include a picture of some way that they will be a steward during the next week, or a promise to spend time helping someone or helping the environment.

- Give an account of the children's offering in the bulletin, including the number of pictures and good deeds, as well as the money.

- Have a special basket at the front of the sanctuary for the children to place their envelopes. Coming forward to do this gives them another opportunity to move about during the service. But do not make it at the same time as the children's message, because then they may feel they can't come forward for the message if they don't have an envelope.

- Form a small committee of children to decide how their offering will be used. Research ahead of time and give them several options.

- To begin using envelopes with children, after a stewardship study ask children to design an envelope. You may want to incorporate some of the drawings in a printed design on envelopes that are used regularly.

seem to understand a little about stewardship, invite them to be a part of your planning team.

3. Begin each meeting in prayer, asking God to guide you as you plan. During the meetings, pause for prayer before each major decision. In this way you will wrap your plans in prayer.

4. As a committee, spend some time studying the biblical background of stewardship. Chapter one of this book can act as a foundation for that study.

5. Review the theme that your church has chosen, or brainstorm possible themes (see below).

6. Decide on the format and time frame. If you have had no real study of stewardship in recent years, then you will need to have several weeks of study. However, if your church has a good grasp of the stewardship lifestyle, then you may want to narrow the time frame and make reference to your past studies. If you choose the same format year after year it can become a "ho-hum" sort of thing that tends to blank out people's minds. Here are a few suggestions.

   • several Sunday school class sessions;

   • one big emphasis on one Sunday;

   • several mid-week study sessions;

   • a church-wide or family study in a Saturday morning or Sunday afternoon retreat setting (see the mini-retreat on page 107);

   • a church-wide or family study in a Friday evening and Saturday morning retreat setting (see the mini-retreat on page 107);

   • a packet of information to send home.

After a concentrated study of stewardship with all children, you may set up a study plan for an in-depth study each year for children of a specific age and review studies for those who have gone through the in-depth study. Since you are likely to have new students in the age levels that will be reviewing the study, be sure to select some activity that defines stewardship, even if you have had stewardship studies in the past.

Using Pledge Cards with Children

Obviously, a child's pledge card will be different from that of an adult's. It should list every activity for which children could volunteer. If there are age limits to a specific volunteer task, then be sure to note that. You might make up a time and talent booklet that lists each item on the pledge card, giving a description of the activity, time it will take, age requirement, the name of the person in charge, any meeting or training times, etc.

Follow up after children turn in a pledge card so they have opportunity to actually do the things they volunteered for.

Here are a few things that might be included on a pledge card. Your own church programs will determine additional items.

- liturgy-related activities such as greeter, acolyte, reader (scripture, litany, etc.), choir member, usher assistant, etc.;

- volunteer in-house time such as stuffing envelopes, helping with younger children, weeding flower beds, raking leaves, sweeping, dusting, setting tables, etc.;

- volunteer mission time such as visiting nursing home, making sandwiches for a food kitchen, bringing food for food pantry or other gifts for needs, etc.

1. Review the stewardship goals for children in chapter two. Keep these before you as you plan.

2. Review the suggestions in this book and select a variety of learning approaches. Try to include methods that are both visual and audio and that use the intelligences discusses on page 12 of this book.

3. For each session you plan, decide on the main idea and purposes.

After your study, include children in the evaluation process by talking with them about what they learned and what learning activities they most enjoyed. This will give you an idea of the methods that might be best to use in future studies.

Possible Themes

Following Jesus' Stewardship Lifestyle
Tithing: Passing God's Gifts to Others
Giving, a Sign of Growth
We Love Because God First Loved Us
We Are the Church Together
Living Simply, That Others Might Simply Live
Living the Life of Stewardship
Stories of Stewardship (emphasizing storytelling)

Developing Stewardship Resources for Families with Children

I have a large silver plated pitcher that was in my family from my earliest recollections. It was usually tarnished and sat on the pantry shelf. Each time my father was paid he would take one-tenth of the amount and place the cash in the pitcher. Each Saturday night, in preparation for Sunday, he would put some of the money in an envelope for church and give us girls some for our offering. We knew from early childhood that this was what we were giving to God through the church.

Most of today's parents struggle with stewardship themselves, and they are certainly at a loss for ways to teach their children. The mini-retreat that follows this chapter offers opportunity for parents and children to explore stewardship together. It also gives parents ideas of ways to help their children at home.

Your committee may want to produce a booklet with suggestions for use in the home. Or you might feature a different family stewardship idea in each copy of your newsletter, or give monthly suggestions on your church web site.

Review the list of resources at the back of this book. Several of them will give you additional ideas, and some may be given to each family.

Bonus:

A Mini-Retreat for Parents and Children Together

THIS RETREAT CAN BE SPECIFICALLY FOR parents and children, or it can be an intergenerational retreat for the whole congregation. If you have adults without children, encourage them to work together in small groups or hook up with a family. The families will each come away from the retreat with a book to remind them of the retreat and of their discoveries about stewardship.

This retreat can be an evening or an afternoon, or it can be part of an extended retreat that includes other subjects. The bulk of the retreat time will be spent in family groups, working at the activity centers. You may choose as many as you like, or explore all of the activity centers. The supply list on page 113 will help you set up the centers. Some of the centers may be placed together on one table, and some may require a table alone. Some centers may use a wall or floor space. Use the information on the Stewardship Activity Center Guide (see page 109) to make small signs for each center so the families can read about them at the tables. Give the Stewardship Activity Center Guide to each family so they can review it and choose which centers they want to do first. There is no special order for the centers.

Schedule

Introduction: discuss the following questions and statements:

- What do you think of when you hear the word "Steward?" (A steward manages the affairs of another or the things that belong to another. Well-to-do persons in the past had stewards who managed their household and other stewards who managed their business.)

- Who made the earth?

- If God made the earth, then what belongs to God?

- What is our job on earth? (We are God's stewards who care for the earth and all that is in it. God gave us abilities and talents to do the job. We were created in God's image, and therefore our care of the earth and all that is in it should take on God's image—and we believe that to be a loving, caring God.)

Scripture: Psalm 24:1

Group Activity:

Pass out pictures and ask each family to discuss how the picture relates to our biblical understanding of stewardship. (These pictures might include scenes of water, litter, an act of caring, animals, trees, etc.)

Activity Centers:

Explain the procedure and assist the families in any questions they have.

Closing:

Ask them to decide as a family and as individuals one thing they will do this next week to become better stewards. Ask them to write that statement on the inside cover of your books and write a date when they plan to have it accomplished.

Shared prayer:

Our God, we've enjoyed this time together.
We've learned much about being a good steward,
and now we're ready to take some action
on what we've learned.
Here are some of the things we plan to do:

Thank you, God, for all the opportunities to be your steward. Amen.

Stewardship Activity Center Guide

Use this activity center guide as you move from one center to another. There is no special order, and you may choose to work in any center you like. Try to spend some time in each center. If time does not allow you to complete each center, take the handouts from those centers you miss so that you can do them at home. Be sure to visit the "Make a Book" center at some point so that you will have a book to take home.

Make a Book

- Select a cover.
- Decide on a title for your book.
- Make the title page, including title, names of persons in the group, date and location.
- Take a picture (or draw a picture) of your family/group and place on a page in book, identifying everyone in the photo.
- Put the book together with brads. You will be adding to the book at other centers.

The Bible Helps Us Know Our Job as Stewards for God

- Look up one or more of the scriptures on the page at the table.
- Paraphrase (put into your own words) the verses on the page for your book.
- Illustrate the verses if you like.
- Place the page in your book.

Tell a Bible Story

- Practice telling this story with motions. One person may read the words and do the motions and everyone else in your group repeats the words and motions after each sentence. This is called echo pantomime.
- Illustrate it for your book if you like.

Make a Prayer Poem

- Decide on the subject for your prayer.
- Using the form on the page, make a prayer (cinquain) poem.
- Pray the prayer together.
- Place the prayer in your book.

Look at God's Creation

- Investigate different items on the table and talk about how we are stewards of God's different creations.
- List on a page the different ways that you can care for God's creation.
- Place the page in your book.

Listen to and Measure Water

- Listen to the sounds of water on the CD.
- Imagine just where you might be when you hear the sounds.
- Use the water and measuring cups to measure 2½ quarts of water that we need every day to maintain a normal water balance in the body.

Read About Water

- Read the page of facts about the use of water. On the back of the paper, list ways that you can be a steward and save water in your home.
- Place the page in your book.

We See How We Are Stewards in Our Community

- Using blocks, set up a community.
- As you build, talk about places where we help to take care of God's creation, such as in our homes, in our yards or gardens, in the parks, by using recycle bins, at bird feeders, and such.
- Thank God for the opportunity to care for creation.

Stewardship of a Car

- Using the page, list the reasons we use a car.
- Discuss the following points:
  - Is each reason a need or a desire?
  - How does each reason affect your family finances?
  - How does each reason affect the time schedule of individuals in the family (particularly the drivers)?
  - Should one reason take priority over another if the car cannot be used for all reasons?
  - What is the definition of stewardship of money and time? Why does this make a difference in the demands that each of us puts on the use of a car?

— What are alternatives for using a car in each situation?
- How would God have us use our cars as stewards?
- Put the page in your book

My Favorite Things

- Follow directions on the page on the table.
- After you have finished and folded the paper and answered the questions on each fold, then discuss the questions at the bottom of the back of the page with your family/group. Talk about how God has given us minds to be able to hold down jobs.

Advertisements

- People write advertisements to try to sell their things. Look at the newspaper and magazine advertisements and read the questions attached. Talk about them with your family or group.
- Look at the checklist of questions to ask yourself while watching television advertisements. What other things might you add to the checklist?
- Put the page in your book to take home and use while watching television.

Poster of a Steward

- On sticky paper, write how you can use a different part of your body to act as a steward. Place the sticky paper signs on the appropriate part of the steward's body.

  Example: Eating an inexpensive meal and sending extra money to others who need food. (Place by mouth.)

- Decide on one specific thing you will do at home to be a better steward.

Make Sign for Home

- Read Joshua 24:15. Joshua decided that he and his family would serve the Lord.
- Decide how you can serve the Lord as a steward and make a sign to place in your home, using the passage from Joshua.

What's a Tithe?

- Read Leviticus 27-30 to see what a tithe was in Old Testament days.
- Today many Christians set aside 10% of what they earn to give to the Lord.
- Use the play money and pass it out randomly among your group. Work together to determine how much is a tithe (10%) for each amount handed out.

At Home after Our Time Together

- Take a page for each person to use when you get home.
- On it, each person will draw what he or she enjoyed most during the evening.
- Share the drawings and thank God for time together.

Supply List for Mini-Retreat for Parents and Children Together

(Note: Make sure that all pages at centers are punched with three holes ahead of time to be placed in their books.)

Make a Book

- Covers cut to paper size, wallpaper, construction paper, etc. Paper with three holes for title page. (Make a sample.)
- Polaroid camera and film or digital camera and computer to print photo.
- Markers, crayons, glue, brads, and three-hole punch if covers aren't punched.

The Bible Helps Us to Know Our Job as Stewards for God

- Page "Bible Verses to Paraphrase," pencils, crayons, markers, three to four Bibles. (See page 121.)

Tell a Bible Story

- Page "The Widow's Gift," crayons and markers. (See page 118.)

Make a Prayer Poem

- "Stewardship Prayer Poem" and pencils. (See page 122.)

Look at God's Creation

- Page "Ways We Care for God's Creations" and pencils. (See page 115.)
- Various pictures on table: plant, trees, animals, water, leaves, flowers, washed out ground, birds, fish, etc.

Listen to and Measure Water

- CD of water sounds (a river, rapids, or raindrops) and player.
- Large container of water, measuring cups, empty gallon container with open mouth to have water poured into from measuring cups.

Read about Water

- "Water Facts" about the use of water and pencils. (See page 116.)

We See How We Are Stewards in Our Community

- Blocks, cars, and people figures.

Stewardship of a Car

- "Stewardship of a Car" and pencils. (See page 117.)

My Favorite Things

- "My Favorite Things" and pencils. Also place a folded sample at the table.

Advertisements

- Advertisements from magazines and newspaper, including luxury items.
- "Advertisement Check List" and pencils. (See page 123.)

Poster of a Steward

- Poster of a "gingerbread man" with eyes, ears, nose, mouth drawn in. Hang it on a wall or lay it on a table.
- Sticky papers and pencils.

Make Sign for Home

- Construction paper, markers or crayons, Bible.

What's a Tithe?

- Bible and play money. One-dollar bills may be easier for them to use.

At Home after Our Time Together

- Blank three-hole paper.

Ways We Care for God's Creation

_____

_____

_____

_____

_____

_____

_____

_____

_____

_____

_____

_____

Water Facts

- No life on earth is possible without water.
- Water provides a home for nearly 90% of all living plants.
- Water covers 75% of the earth's surface, but 99% of the water is either salt water in the oceans or frozen in glaciers.
- If all the glacier ice that exists today melted, a layer of water approximately 196 feet deep would be added to all of the world's oceans — and many coastal lands would be submerged.
- You can live without food for more than a month, but without water for less than a week.
- Every day 1 billion people on earth drink contaminated water.
- 25,000 people die every day for lack of clean drinking water.
- About 80% of all sickness and disease can be attributed to inadequate water or sanitation.
- Although only a fifth of a gallon is all one needs to survive, a person must take in 2½ quarts of water a day to maintain a normal water balance in the body.
- Mothers in some countries walk 15 miles each day for water, sometimes requiring 8 hours a day. In the U.S., on the average, we use 200 gallons of water a day per person.

It takes Water to Make Things

- One Sunday newspaper takes about 150 gallons
- One automobile tire takes about 2,000 gallons
- One slice of bread takes about 37 gallons
- One ton of oil takes about 180 tons of water
- One ton of paper takes about 250 tons of water
- One ton of steel takes about 150 tons of water
- One ton of grain takes about 1,000 tons of water

Source: "Drink from the Well of Living Water" by Alternatives for Simple Living, www.simpleliving.org

Stewardship of a Car

List below the reasons that we use a car.

_____

_____

_____

_____

_____

_____

_____

- Discuss the following points:
  — Is each reason a need or a desire?
  — How does each reason effect your family finances?
  — How does each reason effect the time schedule of individuals in the family (particularly the drivers)?
  — Should one reason take priority over another if the car cannot be used for all reasons?
  — What is the definition of stewardship of money and time? Why does this make a difference in the demands that each of us puts on the use of a car?
  — What are alternatives for using a car in each situation?

- How would God have us use our cars as stewards?

The Widow's Gift

(Echo pantomime based on Luke 21:1-4)

An echo pantomime combines action (pantomime) with words. The leader gives a brief sentence with actions and the group responds (echoes) the sentence and action back.

Words	Actions
One day Jesus was at the Temple.	Shape a Temple with hands over head.
He saw people putting money gifts	Take money from pocket and put in pretend box.
in the offering box.	
Some people were giving lots of money.	Put money in over and over.
But a poor widow only put in	As you count "one . . . two . . . " make two
One . . . two . . . pennies.	deliberate motions of putting in a penny.
Jesus said, "This poor woman	Move one hand out as if pointing to woman and
gave more than all the rest.	with the other make spreading motion for "all."
The others had much and gave little.	Spread arms open wide to indicate "much"
	and shake head to indicate "little."
But she had little but gave all that she had."	Hold hands together and open them to indicate their emptiness, and smile.

My Favorite Things

— Think about all of the things you own personally.

— Decide on your four favorite possessions.

— Write these in the four sections as indicated.

— Turn up the bottom of the page, so that the bottom touches the bottom line.

— Answer the question on the folded paper.

— Continue with each fold line.

- -

Favorite Possession #1

- -

Favorite Possession #2

- -

Favorite Possession #3

- -

Favorite Possession #4

How would I feel if I could not have Possession #4?

How would I feel if I could not have Possession #3?

How would I feel if I could not have Possession #2?

How would I feel if I could not have Possession #1?

  — What makes it possible for me to have these possessions?
  — Why are my parents (am I) able to work to have money to buy
    these possessions?
  — How can I be a good steward about my possessions?

Bible Verses to Paraphrase

Read some of the verses below from the Bible and select at least one to paraphrase (reword in your own words) now for your book. At home, select a different verse each day this week and paraphrase it.

Genesis 1:26

_____

_____

Leviticus 25:23

_____

_____

Psalm 24:1

_____

_____

Psalm 50:10-11, 12b

_____

_____

Haggai 2:8

_____

_____

Luke 16:13

_____

_____

Stewardship Prayer Poem

A steward is one who cares for or manages another's property.

Use one of the words below as the title and write a cinquain (sin cane) poem about the word and stewardship by using the following form and filling in words that express that subject.

Steward
Gifts
Offering
Responsibility
Care

Example:

Steward

God's   property

Caring   Growing   Enriching

Happy in God's service.

Amen

Line 1: A title of one word or one subject.

Line 2: Two words about the subject (either a phrase or separate words).

Line 3: Three verbs that denote action. May end in "ing" or may be phrase of action.

Line 4: Four words telling about the feeling for line one. May also be a phrase.

Line 5: One word that means same as first line (or reuse the first word or *Amen*).

_____

_____   _____

_____   _____   _____

_____   _____   _____   _____

_____

Advertisement Check List

When you watch television or go on the computer web, use this checklist to think about commercials and how we should be good stewards.

☑ What is the commercial really telling me?

☑ If I had this, what difference would it make in my life?

☑ Is this something I need, or something I want?

☑ How long will this (or the pleasure from it) last?

☑ What will I need to give up in order to purchase this?

☑ What else could I purchase for myself with the same amount of money?

☑ What could I do or purchase for others with the same amount of money?

☑ Would the purchase of this be good stewardship of my money?

☑ What would God like me to do about purchasing this?

☑ _____

☑ _____

☑ _____

Resources

Books

Don't Shoot the Horse ('Til You Know How to Drive the Tractor): Moving from Annual Fund Raising to a Life of Giving by Herb Mather.

Fifty Simple Things Kids Can Do to Save the Earth by John Javna and the Earth Works Group.

Giving Together: A Stewardship Guide for Families by Carol A. Wehrheim.

Stewardship in African-American Churches: A New Paradigm by Melvin Amerson.

Curriculum

PowerXpress, Living as Caretakers and Living God's Word—Money and Time—Curriculum (rotation model), United Methodist Publishing House.

Web Sites

Hunger No More, www.hungernomore.org and click on "Children's Activities."

Bread for the World, www.bread.org and click on "learn."

Save Our Streams (SOS), Izaak Walton League http://www.iwla.org/index.php?id=19

United Methodist Committee On Relief (UMCOR) www.gbgm-umc.org/umcor